COURAGEOUS

Burnt Out, Not Broken

A Journey of Faith, Healing, and Renewal

db

DAWN BURNETT

Clovercroft Publishing

**Library of Congress Cataloging-in-Publication Data
is available through the Library of Congress**

ISBN-13: : 978-1-968127-41-1 (Paperback)
ISBN-13: 978-1-968127-54-1 (ePub)

Published by Clovercroft Publishing
Clovercroftpublishing.com

Editing by Christine Belleris
Cover and Interior Design by Larissa Henoch

CONTENTS

ACKNOWLEDGMENTS

This book would not have been possible without the incredible people who walked beside me during one of the most transformative seasons of my life.

First and foremost, thank you to Christine for the co-writing opportunity, your belief in my story, and for helping bring these experiences, lessons, and emotions to life on paper. Your support and creative partnership helped shape this book into something deeply meaningful.

To my guardian angel and to my travel bestie, Traci—thank you for being a safe place during chaos, uncertainty, healing, and transition. Thank you for opening your heart, your patience, and even space for my urgent belongings while I navigated one of the biggest life changes I have ever experienced. So much of this journey would have felt far heavier without your friendship beside me.

To those who helped me pack, move, clear space, lift bins, encourage me, check on me, and remind me to keep going when life felt overwhelming—thank you. Sometimes the smallest acts of kindness become the biggest lifelines.

A very special thank you to the luxury hotels that became far more than places to stay during this journey—especially Conrad Algarve and Hotel Heron, Alexandria, VA—for providing the most gorgeous room upgrades and creating magical spaces where I was able not only to write, reflect, and heal, but also review and complete this book. Your service exceeded every expectation, and I look forward to future returns, as both locations will always hold a very special place in my heart.

Most importantly, thank you to every person mentioned throughout this book. Every conversation, shared story, unexpected connection, lesson, moment of kindness, heartbreak, laughter, and encounter helped shape these pages. Whether you realized it or not, you became part of a journey that changed my life forever.

This experience taught me that life is not truly about destinations, titles, possessions, or perfection—it is about people, connection, growth, courage, and the moments that unexpectedly touch our souls.

I am forever grateful for the journey.

With love and gratitude,
Dawn Burnett

Chapter 1
DO I MATTER?

Every building begins with a blueprint, the plans, and then the foundation for the structure that can last for years and even generations. Lives, too, begin with a blueprint. Obviously, these are not the kind drawn neatly on paper with straight lines and careful measurements, but one shaped quietly in the early years of childhood—through experiences, words spoken and unspoken, and the way love is given—or withheld.

Mine began in a small town of fewer than a thousand people in upstate New York. From the outside, it probably looked like any other idyllic place where families raised children and life moved at a slower pace, like a Norman Rockwell painting. But inside our home, there was anything but an ideal life.

There existed a constant undercurrent of tension that never quite settled.

I was the middle child of five—two sisters and two brothers. In a house that full, you might expect noise and energy and connection. There was noise—but not the kind that comes from laughter and children playing. It was the kind that made you bristle. That rattles your chest. Raised voices. Arguments that flared up and came without warning. The sharp edge of anger that made you freeze because you didn't know what would happen next.

My parents were not people I would describe as having substance abuse issues, but their relationship was deeply unstable. There was betrayal, hurt, and choices that created a constant storm inside our home.

As children, we didn't understand the details. We just felt the impact. When the fighting started, we didn't intervene. We hid: under tables, inside closets. When this happened, I tried to stay as small as possible. I could feel my heart beating out of my chest so loud I thought you could hear it outside. Sometimes I'd go to a small crawl space cut into the wall that became my hiding place—a tiny cubby hole where, in my mind, a different and better life existed.

A place where things were calm.

Where people were kind.

Where I mattered.

There were nights when the noise became too much, when fear overtook silence, and we would yell out from wherever we were hiding: "Stop hurting her!" We never knew what would happen next. It could stop. It could get worse.

But even then, we didn't fully understand what we were witnessing. As children, you don't have the language for those moments. You only know that something isn't right. That something feels unsafe.

The house itself seemed to mirror the instability inside it. We lived in a few places, but the one I remember most was small and worn, with a red exterior and signs of neglect that no one ever quite fixed. The bathroom walls were damaged from water, slowly deteriorating over time. It felt like everything—both inside the house and within the family—was quietly falling apart.

There were other disturbing experiences from those years that shaped me in ways I didn't fully understand until much later. Moments that came from a lack of guidance, from being children left to navigate things we were too young to process.

What I can say is this: When there is no structure, no protection, and no clear sense of safety, children are left to make sense of the world on their own. And often, left to their own devices and without the emotional maturity needed, they get it wrong. They assume responsibility for things that were never theirs to carry.

What I remember most about those years wasn't just the chaos. It was the absence.

The absence of attention.

The absence of comfort.

The absence of feeling like we mattered.

Children are incredibly perceptive. Even when adults think they're hiding things, kids can sense when something is off. But when no one explains it—when no one reassures you—your mind starts filling in the blanks.

You begin to wonder if somehow it's your fault. I spent much of my childhood trying to prove that I was good enough.

Good enough to be noticed.

Good enough to be loved.

Good enough to matter.

But the harder I tried, the more invisible I felt.

It's a strange experience growing up inside a family and still feeling like you don't quite belong there. Like you're standing just outside the room, watching life happen rather than truly being part of it.

Invisible children become very skilled at reading the room.

We learn to anticipate moods.

We learn when to stay quiet.

We learn how to avoid becoming the next target of someone else's anger.

We become observers.

Eventually, we become survivors.

But every child needs somewhere safe. For me, that place was my grandparents' home. They lived about an hour away, but in my memory, it might as well have been on another planet. It was a different world entirely, where people spoke a different language—one of kindness and unconditional love.

We spent nearly every summer there, five kids lined up side-by-side on the living room floor in sleeping bags, our heads close together, whispering and laughing before falling asleep.

It didn't matter that the space was small. It felt like everything we didn't have at home.

Peaceful.

Predictable.

Safe.

My grandmother ran a small upholstery shop out of the basement. She was the kind of woman who quietly held everything together—taking care of the home, supporting her husband, and creating a space where people felt welcome.

My grandfather built Adirondack guide boats by hand. He was a true artisan.

From a young age, we worked alongside him, learning what it meant to build something with care and patience. That was where our work ethic came from—not from lectures, but from watching and doing. It was the best kind of apprenticeship.

Life there followed a rhythm. Every day at four o'clock, work stopped. We gathered on the front porch, and my grandfather would hand each of us a small sip of his beer—a tradition that felt more symbolic than anything else—and we would sit together, talking, laughing, telling stories.

Meals were shared.

Time was shared.

Life was simple.

And in that simplicity, I felt something I didn't often feel anywhere else. I felt seen. I felt valued. I felt like I mattered.

Looking back now, I realize how important that refuge was. Without it, I'm not sure I would have understood what love was supposed to feel like.

But even safe places can't erase the blueprint being formed at home. Childhood has a way of quietly shaping how we see ourselves and the world. It creates patterns—beliefs that follow us long after we leave those environments behind.

When you grow up in a home where love feels inconsistent, you begin to associate your worth with performance.

You try harder.

You achieve more.

You prove yourself over and over again, hoping that eventually someone will say the words you've been waiting to hear: *You matter!*

But those words rarely come the way we hope they will. Instead, the belief settles deeper inside you:

Maybe you just need to do more.

Be more.

Give more.

And so the blueprint begins to guide your life in ways you don't even realize.

You work harder than everyone else.

You stay longer than you should.

You accept less than you deserve.

You keep trying to prove something that was never yours to prove.

All the while, the child inside you is still asking the same quiet question: "Do I matter?"

It took me many years—and many chapters of life—to understand that this question had been shaping my choices all along. Because when you grow up believing you don't matter . . . you spend the rest of your life trying to prove that you do.

Chapter 2
SEARCHING FOR WORTH

When you grow up feeling invisible, you start looking for ways to be seen. You may not even realize you're doing it at the time. It just feels like something stirring inside you—a quiet determination that if you can just find the *right* place, the *right* moment, the *right* version of yourself . . . someone will finally notice. For me, that search began when I was a young teenager.

I don't remember exactly how old I was, only that something caught my attention—an ad for a beauty pageant. Instantly, I felt a spark, a tap on the shoulder, like this was something I needed to do. Some girls grow up dreaming about pageants, watching Miss America on television and hoping to one day be that girl in Atlantic City. That had never been me, but suddenly, the idea of standing on a stage, being seen, being noticed—that felt important.

Maybe this was it. Maybe this was how I would finally matter.

There was just one problem. As I soon discovered, pageants weren't cheap. The entry fees alone were around a couple hundred dollars—money my family simply didn't have. And then there would be the clothes and the makeup. But I would not let dollars and cents stop me. By this time, I had already learned something about myself: If I wanted something, I would find a way to make it happen.

So I started knocking on doors, house after house in my neighborhood, standing on front porches and explaining what I was trying to do.

"Hi! I'm entering a pageant, and I'm trying to raise money for the entry fee. Would you be willing to donate anything to help?" I would say enthusiastically and giving them my best beauty contestant high-wattage smile. I don't remember every conversation, but what I do remember is how people responded.

They were kind. Some were surprised. Some smiled at the effort. A few asked questions. But more often than not, they gave what they could.

Even then, I didn't fully understand what I was doing. But I can see it now—I was learning how to connect, how to ask, how to believe in something enough to put myself out there. I was learning how to sell.

Dollar by dollar, bit by bit, I raised enough to enter.

Then came the dress. In the world of pageants, dresses are everything. They sparkle, they shine, they transform girls into something that looks effortless and beautiful under bright lights. They can be off-the-rack or they can be one-of-a-kind, but usually they are expensive. Very expensive.

Mine was different. I found it in a factory—for five dollars.

It was pink, made of taffeta, with slightly puffy shoulders and a shell-like cut that formed a soft V at the bottom. It wasn't extravagant, but to me, it was everything. It was my chance.

The day of the pageant arrived, and backstage was a world of its own, a beehive buzzing with excitement. Bright lights. Mirrors everywhere. Girls sitting in chairs, beauty tools, brushes, and cans of product everywhere as their hair was styled and their makeup carefully applied.

I stood there among them, getting ready like everyone else, trying to blend in. But inside, I felt something very different. As I looked around the room, a quiet thought settled in: They're all prettier than me. Can they tell I don't really belong here?

No matter how much effort I put into my hair or makeup, I couldn't shake that feeling. It sat heavy in my chest, whispering the same message I had carried since childhood. You are not enough. I could feel that familiar tightening in my chest—the same feeling I had as a little girl, hiding and hoping not to be noticed unless I had done something right. It didn't matter where I was. A stage, a dressing room, a different life. The feeling followed me anyway.

Still, I put on the dress. I felt amazing with it on. I stepped into the moment. I took a deep breath. Stood straight and tall, put my shoulders back and my chin out and told myself *This is my chance.*

And then, just before picture time, everything changed. As I rushed to make it to the stage for the shoot, I stepped on the hem of my dress. In an instant, the fabric pulled tight and ripped straight across the front.

I froze.

My heart dropped. Heat rushed to my face. The one thing I had worked so hard for—the one dress that made me feel like *maybe* I belonged there—was now torn open just seconds before I had to walk out in front of everyone.

This is it! I thought, dejected and embarrassed. It was over before it had even begun. I could feel tears welling up but I was determined not to cry. My face was flushed with embarrassment.

But then something unexpected happened. The other girls saw what had happened, and instead of turning away or whispering, they came toward me.

"It's okay," one of them said quickly.

"Don't worry—we'll fix it!"

Someone ran to grab tape. Another girl held the fabric together. And right there, in the middle of that busy, competitive backstage room, they began taping my dress back together. Piece by piece.

"It's going to be okay," they kept saying.

No one laughed.

No one judged.

They just helped.

Standing there, surrounded by girls who had every reason to see me as competition, something inside of me shifted.

For the first time in my life, I felt seen. Not because I looked perfect. Not because I had won anything. But because, in a moment when I could have been humiliated, people chose kindness instead of contempt or ridicule.

They saw me—and they showed up for me. For a moment, the invisible girl disappeared.

And yet, as powerful as that moment was, it couldn't undo the deeper pattern that had already been set in motion. Because once you learn to look outside yourself for validation, you don't stop after one experience. You keep searching.

For approval.

For recognition.

For proof that you matter.

The pageant didn't fix that question for me. It simply gave me another place to ask it. Do I matter? And without realizing it, I had already begun building a life around trying to find the answer.

Chapter 3
THE SHADOW YEARS—THE NIGHT EVERYTHING CHANGED

I was twenty-two years old when I married my childhood sweetheart. My husband, Todd, had been my best friend for years. In many ways we built our marriage on that friendship. There was happiness between us, but if I'm honest, we were always better friends than lovers. Still, we were happy, at first at least.

In marrying him, I believed I had escaped the chaos of my early life. He didn't carry the same kind of baggage as I had, and I believed marriage would bring the stability I had been searching for. Safety. A fresh start. A life that looked nothing like the one I grew up in. The weight of the past belonged mostly to me, but I hoped that I would be able to shed the instability as I grew into adulthood as a couple, someone to help share the load and responsibilities.

For a while, things felt steady. But when my grandmother died, something inside me shifted. She had recently come to visit us in Florida with my grandfather, traveling down from Saranac Lake, New York, on Amtrak. The visit felt ordinary at the time. We laughed, shared meals, and said goodbye the way families always do, assuming there will be another visit soon.

But another visit was not to be. A few months later, she was gone. They found her sitting in a rocking chair on the front porch of her home. She had passed away quietly. I suppose she was at peace when God took her, but the thought of her being alone when it happened was a picture I couldn't get out of my head. I was not prepared for such a profound loss—you are never ready to lose someone so important—and I didn't understand all the deep emotions I was feeling, the gnawing sadness I couldn't shake.

My grandmother had been my world—my safe place growing up, the person who made me feel loved when life at home felt uncertain. Losing her left a gaping hole in my life that I didn't yet know how to fill. Looking back, I can see that grief made me vulnerable in ways I didn't fully understand at the time.

One night not long after her passing, I went out alone to an Orlando-area nightclub. I had been there before. It wasn't unusual for me to go dancing, and I loved the energy of the place. The music was loud, the room crowded, and in the center of the club was a spinning dance floor that heightened the sense of fun.

I had been there for about an hour, dancing and enjoying the music. It felt like an ordinary night. Until it wasn't. At some point, someone slipped something into my drink.

What happened after that comes back to me only in fragments rather than a clear sequence. I remember feeling disoriented, my body no longer responding the way it should. The room seemed to blur and tilt. My limbs were heavy, like they had weights attached to them.

Then I remember being in a car. I don't know how I got there. Did I walk there? Did someone carry me there? There was a man driving, but I didn't know who he was. Was this a dream? I asked him where we were going.

He answered matter-of-factly, "We're going to my girlfriend's parents' house. They're out of town."

None of this made sense. Why were we going there if she was not there? I didn't understand what was happening. My mind struggled to keep up with the situation unfolding around me. It was like scenes flashing intermittently, and I was not fully aware of anything.

What I do know is this: I was taken off-site. And I was raped.

The details are not important. What stayed with me instead were the words he said afterward: "This is what you wanted."

In that moment, I felt something deeper than fear. I felt confusion. Shame. This was most definitely not what I wanted, yet somehow, I convinced myself that maybe I had done something wrong. That maybe I had allowed this to happen. That maybe it was my fault. I shouldn't have gone to the club. I shouldn't have gone alone. I should have been at home. I should have dressed differently. I should've acted differently. Like so many rape survivors, I put the blame on myself. Who would believe me?

So I didn't call the police. I didn't tell anyone for a long time. Instead, I locked the experience away and carried the weight of it alone. Silence felt easier than explaining something I barely understood myself.

But trauma doesn't disappear just because we refuse to speak about it. It settles quietly into the background of your life, shaping how you see the world. For me, it created a deep struggle with trust. It reinforced a belief I had carried since childhood—that my voice didn't matter, that my pain didn't matter, and that I was expected to endure difficult things quietly.

Nearly a year later, I was working for a small travel company as a concierge when the phone rang. When I picked it up, I heard a voice that made my entire body freeze.

It was him. I didn't remember what he looked like, but I remembered his deep, gravelly voice. I tensed up. I felt like I was in a tunnel. My mouth went dry and my heart raced. I was petrified.

"You're supposed to marry me," he said.

My mind raced. How did he find me? How did he know where I worked? Had he been watching me all this time?

Before I could respond, my boss grabbed the phone from my hand. He knew what had happened and immediately told the man exactly what he thought of him.

Even now, years later, that moment still sends a chill through me.

The assault didn't just change one night of my life. It shaped the way I moved through the world afterward. Trust became difficult. I became fiercely protective of my body and of who I allowed close to me. In some ways, the experience hardened me. In other ways, it made me determined never again to give someone that kind of power over my life.

But at the time, I didn't see it that way. At the time, I simply carried the silence.

Chapter 4
DISAPPEARING AGAIN

I thought leaving my childhood home meant I had escaped the chaos. I believed that once I was grown up and moved out, I would build something different—something peaceful, something loving. A life where I finally felt safe and valued. But life has a way of revealing the lessons we haven't fully learned yet.

I had been with my first husband—my childhood sweetheart—for most of my life. We started dating when we were very young, just kids growing up side-by-side. By the time we married, it felt less like a choice and more like a natural next step.

We were best friends. There was comfort in that. Familiarity. A kind of steady happiness—but not the kind rooted in deep connection. Looking back, we were more companions than partners. We were married for two years.

Not long after the assault that would change me in ways I didn't yet understand, our marriage quietly came to an end. There was no dramatic collapse. No explosive ending. Just a quiet realization that we were no longer meant to continue together. He didn't want me to leave, but I knew staying with him would be a mistake. I had to keep moving, and I didn't want to live a lie.

The divorce was amicable—handled simply, with a paralegal, everything agreed upon. No messy court fights. No property to wrestle over. No children to tie us to one another.

By 1993, that chapter of my life had closed. And before that year was even over, I had already stepped into another one, starting on the other side of the Atlantic Ocean.

I met him in a nightclub in England. I remember the moment clearly. I had just walked up to the bar when I noticed him across the room, standing with a group of friends. There was something about him that drew my attention immediately.

Mark was about five-foot-ten, slender, with mousy brown hair and a polished, almost effortless style. He carried himself with a kind of quiet confidence. Dapper. Composed. The debonair accent that makes Americans swoon. But more than anything, it was his presence—his voice, his energy—that pulled me in.

It felt exciting. New. Different from anything I had known before.

We spent a few days together while I was there, and when I returned home, we stayed in touch. Phone calls turned into something more, and not long after, he flew to the United States to see me.

That's when he said he wanted to marry me. It caught me by surprise, and it was totally unexpected.

Looking back now, everything moved quickly—too quickly. But at the time, I didn't question it. I saw it as a fresh start. A new beginning. A chance to build the life I had been searching for. So, without thinking too deeply about it, I said yes.

What I didn't know then was how much I still didn't understand about myself—and most definitely about him.

At first, things seemed promising. We began building a life together, and I even helped him establish a U.S. branch of the company he had been working for in the U.K. I believed in him. I supported him, and I was invested in the future we were creating.

But over time, something began to shift. It was subtle at first. Then unmistakably, the emotional tone of the relationship started to change. Rather than supportive and feeling like we were in a partnership, the air around us began to feel tense. Conversations that should have felt safe and began as innocuous began to feel loaded and filled with emotional landmines that could set him off. It was impossible to predict how we'd go from point A to point Z.

The verbal abuse came gradually, but once it started, it became part of the landscape. I did what I always did: I adapted. I learned how to compartmentalize—to file things away in my mind so I could keep functioning, keep working, keep showing up in the world as if everything was fine.

From the outside, it may not have been obvious. I appeared healthy and happy. But internally, it was taking a toll—everything does eventually—if not outwardly, then inwardly. My health began to suffer. The constant stress, the emotional strain—it doesn't just stay in your thoughts. It lives in your body.

And still, I stayed. Because by then, the pattern was familiar. I had learned this long before—that survival sometimes looks like shrinking. And so, shrink I did. It was like being back in my childhood home, hiding in the crawl space, making myself as small as possible.

It wasn't all bad. We built a life over the years. We had children—two incredible, beautiful souls who remain the greatest gifts of that chapter of my life. But behind the scenes, the environment continued to deteriorate.

There were moments when clarity would break through—small flashes where something inside me would say, this isn't right. One of those moments came unexpectedly. I was out at dinner with one of his business colleagues. It was a normal evening, casual conversation, nothing unusual—until he said something that stopped me cold. "So," he said, almost offhandedly, "you're the green card."

The words landed like a weight in my chest. In that moment, something shifted. A quiet knowing. A realization that I had not been seen the way I thought I had been. That the foundation I believed I was standing on was not what I had imagined. I was just a quick path to U.S. citizenship. A vehicle.

But even then, I didn't leave. Not yet. Because leaving isn't just about what you know. It's about when you're ready to act on it.

Over time, the tension escalated. I began to sense there was someone else—that he was having an affair. The emotional distance, the behavior, the feeling in my gut . . . all of it pointed in the same direction. But the tipping point came soon enough—a moment I could no longer ignore.

My children were there when they saw him with his hands around my throat. They watched him pinning me against the glass door in the office of our custom-built home.

That was the line in the sand that could not be crossed. Not just for me—but for them.

Something inside me shifted instantly. A clarity I hadn't been able to access before. This wasn't just about me anymore. This was about my children and there was nothing I would not do to protect them.

I called my father and told him I needed help. He didn't hesitate and flew in shortly after.

"Enough," he said. "It's time to get out."

And this time, I listened. I left in April. By June, we were divorced. And by July, I had moved back to upstate New York, starting over once again.

It wasn't easy. Leaving meant walking away from everything familiar—the home, the life we had built as a family of four, the version of the future I had believed in. But it also meant something else.

Freedom. For the first time in a long time, I could breathe.

Looking back now, I can see the pattern more clearly than I could then. I hadn't just left one difficult situation—I had walked into another that mirrored what I already knew. Not because I wanted pain, but because it was familiar. Because somewhere deep inside, I was still trying to answer the same question that had followed me since childhood: Do I matter?

And for a long time, I tried to answer that question by staying.

By enduring.

By shrinking.

But this time, something was different. This time, I left. And in doing so, I took the first real step toward no longer disappearing.

Chapter 5
MY MIRACLE BOY

The turning point in my life didn't come quietly. It arrived in the form of a beautiful baby boy, my son Max.

By that point, I had already been told I couldn't have more children. My health had been compromised, and I had done my best to accept it. My daughter, Tiffany, was nine, and I wanted to give her a sibling, but I had to be realistic. I told myself she would be my only child. At least, that's what I said out loud. But quietly, persistently, I kept praying. I never stopped hoping.

And then, on the very day I was scheduled for kidney surgery, everything changed. I found out I was pregnant.

I can still feel that moment—the disbelief, the confusion, the overwhelming sense that something beyond logic had just stepped in. It didn't make sense medically. It didn't align with anything I had been told. But it was real. Life—where there wasn't supposed to be life. A second chance.

From the very beginning, Max felt like something more than coincidence. His timing was too exact. Too unexpected. Too impossible to ignore. But miracles don't always arrive gently. His delivery was chaotic. At the hospital, something went terribly wrong. The OB-GYN who had secured my delivery at a well-known women's and children's hospital in Central Florida forgot about me. Yes, forgot!

It was the nurses, the sheroes, who finally stepped in—checking on me, managing what they could, preparing me for release. But in the process and the confusion, a critical detail in my chart was missed. I had a severe latex allergy.

When the bandages were removed, my skin came off with them. The pain was immediate and overwhelming—something I can only describe as a kind of shock that takes over your entire body. In that moment, I understood, in the smallest way, what burn victims must endure.

But the physical pain wasn't the hardest part. I couldn't hold my son. There is nothing as important in those moments right after a baby is born to have skin-to-skin contact with its mother. I longed for it. But I could not hold him. Not for days—but for weeks.

In those first moments of his life—moments that are supposed to be filled with bonding and closeness—I was fighting just to stay upright. My body was shutting down. Infection was setting in. I was dangerously close to sepsis.

I remember gripping the edge of the bed, trying to stand, my entire body resisting even the smallest movement. Everything hurt. Everything felt fragile.

It was my general practitioner who saw what was happening. She didn't hesitate. She intervened quickly, administering a powerful antibiotic injection that, in every sense of the word, saved my life. Looking back, I know how close I came to not being here at all.

And yet, even in the middle of that pain—Max was there. A small, steady light in a very dark moment. He brought a kind of joy into our lives that is hard to fully explain. Not loud or overwhelming—but grounding. Anchoring. Like something had shifted. Like I regained something that I had lost.

But life, as I had already learned, doesn't stop testing you just because you've been given something beautiful. The turmoil in my marriage didn't disappear. The environment didn't suddenly become peaceful.

But something *in me* had changed. Max gave me a deeper sense of purpose—one I couldn't ignore.

And then, when he was just two years old, everything changed again. Life does that. Just when you think it is smooth sailing, a storm develops and you are suddenly navigating rough waters.

Max got sick, and at first it seemed like a normal childhood illness. The kind you expect, the kind you're told will pass. But it didn't.

One round of antibiotics turned into another. Stronger antibiotics. Then another. Then another. Five rounds in, and instead of getting stronger, he was getting weaker. I could feel it in my bones. The kind of knowing that doesn't come from a chart or a diagnosis—but from being a mother. Something wasn't right.

Eventually, we were given an answer: severe celiac disease. It is a chronic autoimmune disorder where consuming gluten—a protein found in wheat, barley, and rye—triggers the immune system to attack and damage the lining of the small intestine. This damage prevents nutrient absorption and can cause serious, long-term health issues if not treated.

Max's body was attacking itself. And the hardest part? There was no clear solution. No real guidance. No sense that anyone was going to fix this for us. I felt like we were finding our way through a dense fog with no help. How were we going to deal with this?

And in that moment, something inside me made a decision. I would not wait for someone else to save my son. I would do whatever it took to get answers. So, I did what some would consider irrational and risky. I walked away from everything. My career in travel. My work in real estate. No work meant no income. No income meant no sense of stability.

None of it mattered anymore. Max was the only thing that mattered.

I went back to school and immersed myself in the study of alternative medicine—determined to understand how the body heals, how the mind and body connect, and what had been overlooked in the traditional paths we had already tried.

I wasn't doing it for a degree. I was doing it for my child.

I studied relentlessly. I was focused in a way I had never been before. This wasn't ambition—it was necessity. His life depended on it.

I graduated with a 4.0. But more importantly, I began to find answers. Along the way, I connected with a medical doctor from France who had developed a formulation designed to support immune healing. Combined with what I was learning, we began to build a new path—one rooted in knowledge, intuition, and a refusal to accept that this was the end of the story.

Step by step, we started to rebuild Max's health. Slowly, carefully, consistently. And then something remarkable happened. He began to get better. Not just managed. Not just stabilized. Better.

His body responded. His strength returned. The child I feared I was losing began to come back to me.

And in the process, something else happened: I began to come back to myself.

What I learned through that journey wasn't just about illness or recovery. It was about power. The kind of power we don't always realize we have—the ability to question, to learn, to advocate, to refuse to accept limits when something deeper tells us there's another way.

Max was my miracle, but he was also my awakening. He pushed me into a level of courage I hadn't accessed before. He forced me to trust myself in ways I never had. He showed me that love—real, unwavering love—doesn't wait for permission.

It acts.

It searches.

It fights.

He didn't just change my life. He transformed it. And from that point forward, one truth became clear: I would never again underestimate the power of a mother on a mission.

Chapter 6
THE NIGHT THE WORLD STOPPED

It was early evening, around five o'clock, in Fayetteville, New York. It was the night before Halloween in 2009, and the town was dressed up for the holiday. Jack-o-lanterns and festive decorations beckoned from porch fronts. A light mist hung in the air. The roads were clear but damp, the kind of quiet autumn evening when everything feels ordinary as people leave work and make their way home for dinner.

I was driving my new white Chrysler Town & Country minivan down the main road that runs through town. My five-year-old son, Max, was in the back seat. We were heading toward the subdivision where my daughter was spending the evening at one of her cheerleading teammates' houses. She had just been named captain of the squad, and the excitement of it still lingered in the air. Max was excited about Halloween as we discussed how we would get his costume together and what kind of candy he was hoping to get tomorrow.

I pulled up to a stoplight and pressed my foot on the brake, waiting for it to turn green so I could make a left turn into the neighborhood.

I didn't know it at the time, but as we were happily conversing, a car was barreling straight for us at fifty miles per hour. He was drunk. We were his brakes.

He slammed into us with a violent bang. Metal crunched. The force snapped my head backward into the driver's seat. My knees were pushed up into the dashboard, my hands jammed against the steering wheel. Airbags deployed just as violently, and I was covered with the powder they released.

Then everything went dark. And strangely . . . calm.

I remember feeling as if I had slipped into another dimension, detached from the pain and chaos that must have surrounded me. My body felt distant, as though it belonged to someone else.

Somewhere in that quiet space, I heard a woman's voice. "Open your eyes."

I didn't recognize the voice, and I had no idea where it was coming from.

"Open your eyes," she said again. Her voice grew stronger and her tone more urgent.

Suddenly, I felt a rush, like I was being pulled sharply back into my body. I opened my eyes just in time to see oncoming traffic heading straight toward me.

"Turn right," said the woman. I jerked the wheel to the right. The van lurched away from the road just as the cars sped past. That was the last time my totaled car would ever run again.

A woman with brown hair jumped out of her car and rushed toward me to help. My mind struggled to catch up with what had happened. My head was twisted back against the seat, and the roof had collapsed behind me.

My first thought was simple: *Am I alive?* No one could survive with their head twisted like this. And then something else hit me. I had forgotten my son! I couldn't turn my head, but I caught sight of the back seat in the rearview mirror. Max was standing there.

Then I heard his voice. "Mommy . . . are you okay?"

For a moment my mind struggled to process the word. *Mommy. I have a son.*

Adrenaline flooded my body. The witness helped open my door, and when I stood up my entire body felt like it was on fire. My hands brushed against broken glass from the shattered windows as we made our way around the van. Cars honked and rushed past us.

Max's door was jammed shut, but we managed to pry it open just enough. Because he was so small and skinny, I was able to pull him out.

We ran across two lanes of oncoming traffic and collapsed on the side of the road. Within minutes paramedics arrived.

Even then, the instinct to protect my son took over. I coached him through everything—how to stay calm, how to lie still as they placed him on the body board.

Inside the ambulance, another paramedic held my phone.

"Lucky you had an OtterBox on this," he said. "Otherwise, it would've been destroyed." He explained he found my phone in the back of the crunched-up van, ringing, and picked it up; it was my daughter. He was familiar with her location only because the son of her teammate's mother had played ball with his son. He was able to give my daughter and the mother directions, and he said she was on her way.

After the hospital cleared my son, we stepped outside into the night. The same mother came to pick us up. We barely knew anyone in town. But somehow, we had made it through.

The recovery was slow. For weeks, I could barely move my arms. But I had one class left to finish my degree in alternative medicine, and I had already earned a 4.0 GPA. So I kept going. Mind over matter.

Three months later, in February 2010, I walked across a stage at Everglades University in Boca Raton, Florida, to receive my degree. It was a picture-perfect sunny day near the water.

For the first time in my life, both my mother and father were there. My father stood with his wife and congratulated me. My mother approached separately. She hugged me for a long time.

Longer than usual.

I welcomed the embrace, but I remember thinking, *Mom, it's not like you're never going to see me again.*

But that's exactly what happened. It was the last time I ever saw her; she passed away with breast cancer and undetected thyroid disease. Nobody knew she was sick.

Looking back now, I understand that October night in Fayetteville—and the quiet hug that followed months later—marked a turning point in my life.

It was the moment I realized that everything I had survived needed to serve a purpose.

Chapter 7
TURNING PAIN INTO PURPOSE

In every healing journey, you come to a fork in the road where you must make a choice. You can carry your pain like something that defines you . . . or you can transform it into something that serves others. That moment came for me not long after I left my marriage.

I was still rebuilding. Still raw. Still trying to make sense of everything I had just walked away from. And then, as if life needed to sharpen the lesson even further, my life was shattered, literally and figuratively, when I was rear-ended by the drunk driver.

That nightmare had a purpose. It forced everything into focus. Life felt fragile. Temporary. Unpredictable. And somewhere in the middle of that uncertainty, a question surfaced: *What is all of this for?*

I didn't want my story to end at survival. I wanted it to mean something. If I had lived through years of chaos, loss, rebuilding, and reinvention, then there *had* to be a reason. Not in a way that justified the pain—but in a way that allowed it to become useful.

That idea changed everything. It started simply. I began sharing stories. At first, they were my own reflections on healing, resilience, and the messy process of finding your way back to yourself. But over time, those stories expanded. They became a safe space for other women as well.

A place to be seen.

A place to be heard.

A place to realize they weren't alone.

From there, the work grew. I started writing more intentionally, shaping my experiences into something others could connect to. What began as personal expression evolved into published books—three in total—each one exploring different layers of healing, courage, and self-discovery. Writing gave structure to what had once felt chaotic. It gave meaning to what had once just been pain.

But words on a page weren't the only way I needed to express it. Music found its way into the mix too. Songwriting became another outlet—another way to process what I had lived through. In time, I released six songs, each one carrying pieces of my story in a different form.

There's something powerful about creative expression. It takes what lives inside you—often unspoken and authentic—and turns it into something that can reach someone else. Someone who is suffering in silence and doesn't know where to turn. Something that can connect. And connection . . . changes things.

One of those connections led to an opportunity I never expected. I became a co-author with Jack Canfield, whose co-authorship of The Chicken Soup for the Soul series inspired millions around the world. To be part of something alongside him felt surreal—a full-circle moment that reminded me how far I had come. The very experiences I once wished I could erase were now opening doors.

Around that same time, I felt called to do something bigger. Something that wasn't just about my voice—but about creating space for others. That's when I launched the #SHERO Project.

It was built on a simple but powerful idea: When women share their stories, something shifts. The project partnered with Thrive Global, expanding the reach and impact. Together, we created a platform where women could speak openly about their experiences, support one another, and reclaim their strength.

Because when women realize they're not alone, shame begins to dissolve. And in its place, something stronger emerges: Courage.

At the same time, I stepped into another arena—producing and hosting online television shows focused on transformation, healing, and personal growth. The response was powerful.

The series grew, and over time it received twenty-six online television awards for production and hosting. On the surface, it looked like success. Recognition. Validation. But even that came with a lesson.

Despite the awards, I was never given the physical trophies by the network owner. For a moment, it stirred something familiar—the old feeling of working hard for something meaningful, only to have someone else control the outcome. But this time, I saw it differently.

The awards were never the point. The real impact wasn't something that would sit on a shelf gathering dust. It was in the messages I received from women who will forever live in my heart. There were the women who reached out to say they felt less alone. Others who said that my work convinced them to finally find the courage to leave a toxic relationship. And the women who decided, maybe for the first time, that they were worthy of more.

That was the real work. That was the real reward.

And still, I had to be honest with myself. Part of my drive during that time was still connected to an old pattern—the need to prove that I mattered. The books. The songs. The recognition. They were, in some ways, evidence: proof.

But underneath that, something deeper had taken root. This wasn't just about being seen anymore. It was about helping others see themselves.

That's when everything became clear. Every chapter of my life—every difficult, painful, complicated moment—had value. The childhood trauma. The relationships that broke me. The struggles that forced me to rebuild from nothing.

None of it was wasted. It was all material. All fuel. All part of something bigger than me.

Because when you turn pain into purpose, it stops being something that defines your past and becomes something that shapes someone else's future.

That is the kind of legacy I wanted to create.

Chapter 8
THE LEAP

I had an almost three-decade long career at a job many people would find interesting and fulfilling. It was. Until it wasn't. For twenty-six years, I worked in the travel industry, and most of that time with one of the largest travel corporations in the world. From the outside, it looked like a great career. The paychecks were good, and the opportunities seemed endless—lots of travel to exotic places at big discounts. I never had to scrimp and save in that regard.

But, as with most things, the truth was more complicated. The industry—especially the side of it I worked in—was intensely competitive and pressure-filled. Every day revolved around numbers, meeting quotas that were always evolving. In sales, you are only as good as your last deal, and every week brought a new expectation to perform better than the one before.

After twenty-five years in this same role, I was eventually being moved into a marketing position. That kind of longevity is rare in the industry. Most people don't last nearly that long because the pressure is so intense. For years, I pushed through the strain and tension because that's what I had always done in life: work harder, prove my value, keep going no matter what. I never asked for anything for myself or to take a step back because I wanted to keep my job and that meant being a team player, not a complainer.

But eventually, my body started sending signals that something was wrong. The first warning came suddenly—a serious kidney issue that required emergency surgery. It was especially frightening because years earlier, in 2000, I had already survived major reconstructive kidney surgery.

Then, about a year later, another health crisis hit. A blood clot. At the time, I was still chained to a desk for long hours, pushing myself to keep up with the demands of the job even when my body was begging for rest. As they say, "sitting is the new smoking," and being parked at my workstation with an elevated heart rate was the worst thing I could have done.

In sales and marketing, everything depends on what we call "leads." A lead is essentially a contact generated through marketing efforts—a potential customer the company can reach out to by phone or email. Those leads are the lifeblood of the business. Without them, you can't produce results. And suddenly, through no fault of my own, the leads coming my way started changing. This was not good, and my numbers began to drop.

In an industry where performance metrics define your value, that shift changed everything. I realized I couldn't just gut my way out of this, so I began asking management for help.

"I just need more training," I told them. "Help me understand what I'm missing."

They did offer some training, but the reality was something everyone in the industry quietly understands: leads are not always distributed equally. Favorites exist. Certain people receive stronger opportunities than others.

It's a bottom-line business, so I tried my best to adapt, but something inside the company had clearly shifted. Management turnover was constant, and the way the business was being run kept changing. After decades of proven performance, I found myself struggling to regain momentum.

I didn't want to lose the seniority I had accrued, so I started applying for other positions within the company. I interviewed for several roles. Every time I made it through the interview process, I felt hopeful.

Every time the answer was the same. No. I was crestfallen but nevertheless determined.

At one point, I applied for a copywriting position—something that perfectly matched my creative strengths. After two interviews, I felt confident the role might finally be the fresh start I needed. Then I received the news that the position had been put on hold due to funding.

Later, when I logged into the company's internal application portal, I was flabbergasted when I saw a note indicating that the lack of funding excuse was a convenient excuse. I had never been considered a realistic hire for the role.

That was the moment something became painfully clear. It felt like someone had stealthily placed a block on my ability to transfer within the company. If what I feared was true, I wanted answers—a valid explanation. I felt I deserved it, after all. I went directly to management.

"If I am not what you were looking for in this role, can you help me find a position in the company that better fits my skills?" I asked.

The answer was simple. "No."

The writing was on the wall. The message was unmistakable: They wanted me out.

Meanwhile, my financial situation was quietly and quickly unraveling. For the first time in my life, I couldn't keep up with the bills. My house payments fell into arrears, and the $25,000 I had built up in savings slowly disappeared as I tried to stay afloat. I didn't want to lean on credit cards, which would make me spiral even further.

In retrospect, I stayed too long. Like someone trapped in a bad relationship, I kept believing things would change if I just worked harder. But they didn't, and I had some difficult choices to make.

Eventually, I was forced to face bankruptcy—one of the most humbling experiences of my life. With the help of a good attorney, I was able to protect the two things that mattered most: my car and my home.

The bankruptcy was discharged in April of 2025. But even after that, I stayed. The company moved me into another department with promises of earning potential that never materialized. I kept applying for new roles internally, hoping for a fresh start. It was the same frustrating story; every application was rejected.

By July of 2025 the message was impossible to ignore. It was time to leave. So, on July 7th, I resigned. And then reality hit. Hard.

Around that same time, something unexpected had begun to take shape in my life—a new idea that would eventually become my own wine brand. The inspiration came from an old nickname. A friend of mine in Toronto had jokingly called me "Burnt Out Party Girl" for years. After two years of hearing it, he finally said one day, "If you don't do something with that name, I will."

At first, I laughed it off. Then life took me to Cascais, Portugal. While I was there, I met an illustrator named Sahil from Vancouver. I told him my idea. We stayed in touch after I returned home.

A month later, he sent me a piece of artwork he had been working on—an illustration in the style of an old sailor tattoo. It featured a striking woman designed for what he thought might be merchandise tied to the nickname.

But when I saw the image, a completely different idea formed in my mind. "That's the wrong woman," I told him. "This is going to be a wine brand." That moment changed everything.

In October of 2024, I began working on trademarking the name. By December I was in discussions with an Italian winery, although importing and distribution proved complicated. Then, in January of 2025, while attending the Scottish Highland Games in Winter Springs, Florida, in search of press coverage, I met the New York winery that would eventually become my partner.

By April of 2025 the labels were officially registered. The brand had launched. But the most important part of the brand wasn't the wine itself. A portion of every bottle sold supports the organization RAINN, the Rape, Abuse, & Incest National Network, which helps survivors of sexual assault. The commitment is printed directly on the back of every label.

For me, the brand represented more than a business. It was a way to transform pain into purpose. Even with the new venture taking shape, the financial pressure continued building. I applied to 180 jobs in six months. Two interviews. Zero offers.

It felt as if the universe was forcing me toward a path I hadn't fully planned. I needed to sell the house.

Chapter 9
SELLING THE HOUSE AND LETTING GO—BURNT OUT, NOT BROKEN

At some point, the things we build begin to define us. A home. A career. The routines that quietly shape our days and give us a sense of stability. Over time, they stop feeling like choices and start feeling like identity.

For years, my home represented exactly that. It was something I had worked incredibly hard to create as a single mother—a place where my son grew up, where memories were made, where I proved to myself that no matter what life handed me, I could rebuild. When I purchased the property for it, I proudly stood in front of the sign announcing it and posted a picture on social media for all to see. I was over the moon.

But there's a difference between stability and attachment. And eventually, life asks you to see it.

Selling my house wasn't just a financial decision. It was an emotional reckoning. It meant letting go of something I had fought to hold onto through bankruptcy, hardship, and years of rebuilding. It meant admitting that the life I had worked so hard to maintain was no longer the life I was meant to live. Life is changing.

So, I sold it. In January 2026, I had a cash offer in hand.

With the house sold and my old career behind me, I made a decision that would reshape my life completely: I would become a digital nomad.

Not just traveling for adventure—but searching for clarity, purpose, and the answer to a question that had followed me quietly through every chapter of my life: What was I truly meant to do here?

Just like that, everything began to simplify. What had once filled an entire home was reduced to what I could justify keeping. The rest was donated, released, or stored. Years of accumulation distilled into two 10 x 20 storage units. At fifty-six years old, I stood in front of those doors and realized something that might terrify most people: I no longer had a permanent address. But what I felt wasn't fear: it was freedom.

In the weeks that followed, as I began traveling, I noticed a pattern in the conversations I was having with people. I'd tell them about what I'd done and they'd get a surprised look and say, "So . . . you're homeless?" The question always came with a mix of curiosity and concern.

I would smile and reply, "No, I'm not homeless."

Homelessness is a lack of choice. This was the opposite. I had chosen this—at least for as long as it made sense. It was a conscious decision to step outside the life I had known and explore something different. I had places to land, keys to friends' homes, and a plan that allowed me to move between them with ease.

It wasn't rootless. It was intentional.

What most people didn't see was the preparation behind it. Months of sorting through everything I owned. Letting go of what no longer served me and being honest about what did. Reviewing my finances carefully to make sure this chapter was sustainable. Mapping out travel, logistics, and the small but important details that create stability within movement.

I updated legal documents. Made sure my trust and executor were in order. Secured important contracts. Updated emergency contacts. Purchased comprehensive travel insurance.

I even thought through the scenarios no one wants to consider—what happens if something goes wrong far from home and I get sick . . . or worse.

This wasn't impulsive. It was deliberate.

The truth is, if I had wanted to return to a more traditional life, I could have done so at any time. I could have rented an apartment, settled back into routine, and rebuilt something familiar. But for the first time, I allowed myself to question whether that familiar path had ever truly been mine.

So instead, I stepped onto a plane, and something shifted. This wasn't a vacation. It wasn't a break from real life.

It was a different way of living it.

Over the months that followed, I moved across the country and eventually through Europe. I met people I never would have encountered otherwise. Conversations with strangers turned into moments of clarity. New environments offered perspective that years of staying in one place never had.

Travel strips life down. When everything you need fits into a suitcase, you begin to see what actually matters. Not the house. Not the things. Not the image of success you've been taught to chase. What remains is something simpler.

Presence.

Connection.

Experience.

And the realization that there is no single way to live a meaningful life—only the one that feels true to you.

This journey wasn't about escape. It was about reclamation. Reclaiming the parts of myself that had been buried under years of responsibility, survival, and the quiet need to prove my worth. At fifty-six, I gave myself permission to live differently.

To move.

To explore.

To exist without the labels I had carried for so long.

In doing so, I proved something to myself that I had spent a lifetime questioning: After everything I had endured, everything I had built, and everything I had let go of, I was still capable of beginning again.

This wasn't a sabbatical. It was a decision. A refusal to keep living a life that no longer fit—and the beginning of one that finally did.

Chapter 10

CHOOSING TO BE SEEN

Even now, I still feel it—the quiet pull of the shadows.

It hasn't disappeared just because I've done the therapeutic work. Healing doesn't grant you a clean break from the past, and growth doesn't erase what shaped you. The echoes of childhood—the fear, the abandonment, the subtle, persistent belief that you don't matter—don't simply dissolve. They linger at the edges. They surface in moments of doubt. They tighten their grip right before you're about to take a risk, to step forward, to be seen.

For a long time, I misunderstood that. I thought those feelings meant I was failing somehow—that I hadn't healed enough, that I wasn't strong enough, that there was still something broken inside me I hadn't managed to fix. I measured my progress by the absence of fear, and when it didn't disappear, I turned on myself.

But I see it differently now.

Feeling like you don't matter isn't proof that you don't. It's evidence that, at some point, you were never taught that you do. There is nothing wrong with you. There never was, even if you didn't know it.

That realization didn't magically silence the voice—but it changed my relationship to it. It gave me distance. It gave me choice. Because if something was learned, it can be unlearned. And if it can be unlearned, it can be replaced—with something truer, something chosen.

That's where everything began to shift. Not with a grand declaration or a dramatic turning point, but with a decision so quiet it almost felt insignificant: I would keep showing up. Every day. Each morning was the chance for a new beginning.

Some days, showing up looks like courage—speaking, risking, stepping into spaces that once felt off-limits. Other days, it looks like discipline—doing the work even when I'd rather retreat and shrink. And sometimes, it's far less glamorous. Sometimes it's simply getting out of bed and choosing, deliberately, not to disappear.

I started giving myself a simple structure: five steps a day toward my goals. Nothing overwhelming. Nothing performative. Just five intentional moves forward, no matter how small they seemed. Because I've come to understand that progress isn't built on perfection. It's built on presence.

And for the first time in my life, I'm choosing to be present in my own story. I'm choosing visibility over silence.

For so long, silence felt like safety. It kept me hidden, protected from judgment, from rejection, from the vulnerability of being fully known. But it also kept me small. It kept me contained within a version of myself that was easier to manage, easier to explain, easier to ignore.

Now I understand something I didn't before: I matter not because of what I've survived. I matter because I keep growing and becoming, no matter what. I refuse to stop becoming. That distinction changed everything.

Survival is where the story begins. Becoming is where it continues.

And this chapter—this next stretch of my life—is about choosing that continuation with intention.

I made the decision to become a nomad for a few months. Not as an escape, not as a pause from real life, but as a conscious step *toward* it.

I made the intentional decision to stop organizing my choices around fear, scarcity, or someone else's definition of what a successful life is supposed to look like.

For years, I followed the blueprint. Someone else's plan for my life. I did what you're supposed to do. Built what you're supposed to build. Checked the boxes that signal you're on the right path.

And still, something felt off. Because the life I was constructing didn't fully belong to me. It belonged to expectation—to inherited ideas about stability, achievement, and worth.

So, I stepped away. Into the unknown. Into discomfort. Into something more honest than anything I had been living before. And then, in the middle of that transition, something small but significant happened—a minor medical diagnosis.

On paper, it wasn't catastrophic. It didn't come with dramatic consequences or immediate urgency. But internally, it landed differently. It interrupted me. It forced stillness. It asked a question I could no longer ignore. What happens if I don't have the option for putting things off, waiting for later? It hit me: tomorrow is not promised.

It's a phrase we all know how to say. It's much harder to actually feel.

In that moment, the illusion of "later" lost its grip. The idea that there would always be more time—to start, to risk, to live more fully—suddenly felt fragile.

We tell ourselves we'll do it later. When things calm down. When we feel more prepared. When it feels safer. But what if later never arrives? That question didn't scare me. It clarified me.

So, I made another decision—firmer this time, less negotiable. I will not play small anymore. Not in my voice. Not in my dreams. Not in the way I participate in my own life. I am choosing visibility over safety. Faith over fear. Purpose over appearance.

The truth is, playing small doesn't actually protect you. It limits you. It edits you down. It trains you to believe that your life should be manageable instead of meaningful, that your desires are excessive, that your voice is optional.

And I've learned—slowly, and not without resistance—that the cost of shrinking is far greater than the risk of being seen.

So, I'm all in. Creatively. Spiritually. Professionally. Not halfway. Not cautiously. Not waiting for some future version of myself to feel ready enough. Fully.

If the question is: *Do you feel like you matter?*—then this chapter is my answer. Not in what I say, but in how I live. In the choices I make. In the risks I take. In the way I keep moving forward, even when the shadows are still there, still whispering, still trying to pull me back into something smaller.

I matter.

Not because someone finally told me I do. But because I decided to believe it. And that decision isn't something I made once.

It's one I make—quietly, deliberately—every single day.

Chapter 11
THE NOMAD YEARS

People often think that the hardest part of starting over is selling your house. That might be true for some people, but it wasn't the house itself—it was everything inside it and letting go. By the time I made the decision to change my life, I had accumulated years' worth of belongings—filling a 2,138-square-foot home and a two-car garage. Boxes stacked on boxes. Furniture, décor, electronics, clothes, kitchen gadgets, artwork. A life measured in things.

Each item carried a story. Something I had worked for. Some souvenirs from a great vacation. Something I had justified keeping even though I really didn't need or use it. Something I put away and had forgotten. Something I might need . . . someday. That was always the reasoning. Before you know it, I had accumulated all these pieces of my life.

Growing up in poverty leaves a mark that doesn't easily fade. Even as an adult, even after building a life for myself, there was always a quiet voice in the background: *What if you can't afford to replace this? What if you need it later?*

Scarcity has a way of disguising itself as practicality.

For years, I listened to that voice. Until I couldn't anymore.

My spiritual teacher had been gently planting the seed. "Let go of the stuff," she would say. "It's weighing you down."

At first, I resisted. I had worked too hard for these things. Letting them go felt like erasing proof that I had built something—that I had made it out of where I came from. But the more I looked around, the more I saw something else.

Not success. Weight. An anchor.

Everything I owned required something from me—attention, maintenance, space, energy. Cleaning it. Organizing it. Moving it from place to place. My possessions weren't supporting my life. They were anchoring it. I didn't pay for them just once, either. Every move cost me money. Not to mention time.

So I made a decision. I would let it go.

Not all at once. I didn't have the capacity for that kind of emotional detachment overnight. But slowly, intentionally—one drawer, one closet, one box at a time—I began sorting through everything I owned.

It was always a decision. What should stay. What should go. What mattered. What didn't.

In total, I donated more than eighty-five bags, boxes, and bins of belongings—items worth thousands of dollars—to the Breast Cancer Awareness Foundation in honor of my mother.

I wouldn't have believed it at first, but giving it away changed everything. Selling would have kept me tied to the value of the items. Donating allowed me to release them.

There were things most people would have held onto—a 62-inch flat-screen TV, furniture, artwork, mirrors, a grill, entire rooms worth of household items. Things that once felt important. Things that no longer did.

The goal became simple: My entire life needed to fit into two storage containers. Just two.

A few seasonal items stayed with close friends so I could move between places more easily, but everything else had to go. At first, it felt unnatural. I had spent years accumulating. Now I was deliberately and rapidly releasing.

But as the house began to empty, something shifted. I felt lighter. Not just in my space—but in myself. Every object I let go of seemed to carry something with it. Old memories. Old identities. Versions of me that no longer fit who I was becoming.

I realized I wasn't just clearing out a house. I was clearing out my past. Especially the parts I hadn't fully processed—the pain from my marriage, the weight of everything I had carried for so long without even realizing it.

Once everything was sorted, donated, and packed away, I locked the storage units. Just like that, the life I had spent years building had been reduced to what could fit inside two boxes.

And then I left. I would be going to . . .

California.

Miami.

Orlando.

Virginia.

New York.

And eventually, five weeks traveling through Europe.

When you live out of a carry-on and a single suitcase, your perspective changes quickly. You start asking a different question: *What do I* actually *need?* The answer surprised me. Very little.

With everything else stored away, I found myself worrying less—not more. I had taken the practical steps to protect what I kept, but mentally, I was free from it.

And in that space, something unexpected emerged: Time.

Minimalism, I realized, isn't about having less. It's about having more of what matters. More time for people. More space for experiences. More presence in your own life.

Without the constant pull of things needing attention, I could finally be where I was—fully.

One simple practice helped me along the way: before letting go of something meaningful, I would take a picture of it. Why? Because it's rarely the object we're attached to. It's the memory of that object. The blanket you and your child would cuddle under while you watched TV. The piece of pottery you got at a weekend art show you visited with your friends. Once I understood that, it became easier to release the physical form without feeling like I was losing the meaning.

Letting go didn't leave me empty. It left me free.

Now, when I travel, I bring only a few small items—tokens of gratitude, reminders of where I've been and what I've come through. Not because I need them, but because I choose them. There's a difference.

The truth is, when you own a lot of things, those things quietly begin to own parts of you. You think about them. Maintain them. Protect them. Worry about them. They take up more than space. They take up energy. They take up time.

And the older I get, the clearer it becomes: Stuff doesn't create happiness. Connection does.

Experiences.

Relationships.

Moments shared with the people we love.

Those are the things that stay. Those are the things that matter.

And now, with less to carry, I finally have more room for all of it. Suitcase in hand, the world open in front of me, I understand something I didn't before: Letting go isn't loss. It's freedom.

Chapter 12

THE DAY EVERYTHING FIT INTO TWO BOXES

Thursday, February 26, 2026. This was the day it all became real. It was a series of endings but a new beginning—a fresh start.

As with most big changes, it was bittersweet. The relationship I had been in for four years had finally come to a clear end, no going back. The house I loved—the one I had worked so hard to buy and had raised my son in—had officially closed. I signed the endless pile of papers and I handed over the keys. It was time for new owners to create their own memories.

When the dust settled after a frantic month of culling and donating and disposing, everything I owned fit into two 20'-by-10' storage units with a few scattered items stored at two friends' homes so I could navigate the beginning of my new nomadic life.

Just like that, my life had been reduced to what could fit inside two boxes—albeit big ones. It was shocking but also liberating realizing how little we really need, how we spend so much of our precious time supporting our possessions, our "stuff."

There were many moving parts leading up to that moment. Rehoming my dog with a good friend. Racing through appointments.

Thirty exhausting days of planning travel, terminating utilities, repositioning my work, and packing up the contents of a 2,138-square-foot home.

From the outside, the idea of floating freely through life might sound exciting—almost glamorous. But freedom comes with sacrifices. Every step of the process required precision. I truly felt guided by my spirits—my guardian watchers—through each decision. If I had held onto even one more unnecessary possession, something driven by the scarcity mindset I developed growing up in poverty, the boxes wouldn't have closed so perfectly.

Hoarding things once felt like security to me. Now letting them go felt like liberation.

That evening ended with one final dinner—the symbolic closing of a four-year chapter. As the night unfolded, the familiar patterns of selfish behavior I had seen so many times before surfaced yet again. In that moment, clarity washed over me.

It was time. Time to move forward.

I booked a hotel in a tourist area nearby. The next morning, I woke up early, headed to the airport, and boarded a flight to California. Three top wineries I had met at a major wine event in New York City had invited me to interview them.

For a moment, the trip felt like the perfect escape.

Each evening, I sat beside my personal fire pit, a glass of wine in hand, typing away on my laptop as I crafted what I believed to be the perfect reporter's story about each winery's vision and experience.

For a few days, I almost forgot about the reality I had left behind in Central Florida.

After catching up on much-needed rest and reflecting on my journey, I boarded another flight back to Florida, this time to Miami for another major industry wine event.

But travel has a funny way of keeping you humble. When I arrived at the well-known hotel hosting the event, my room keycard refused to work. After several trips up and down three floors trying to resolve the issue, I finally surrendered.

I realized that when the universe is trying to tell you something, you listen. Sometimes surrender is the only option.

I settled into the temporary entrapment of my room and decided the key situation could wait until morning. After all, travel mishaps are practically a rite of passage when you've declared yourself a digital nomad bouncing quickly between locations. I'd need to learn to adapt and make decisions on the fly.

After three incredible days immersed in the wine world, I made my way back to Central Florida. I had booked a stay at a resort villa, hoping it would provide a peaceful escape. But the moment I landed and got into my car, a pit formed in my stomach. Strangely, although I hadn't been away that long, Orlando no longer felt like home.

I stopped at the grocery store to stock up so I could cook healthy meals in my villa. I leaned into gratitude for the simple luxuries—like having a washer and dryer to do laundry. Small things suddenly felt like blessings.

As the days passed and I met my professional commitments, I couldn't help but reflect on something strange. I was always busier in Florida than I ever was in New York or New Jersey. How was that possible? Florida was supposed to be slower paced—the place people moved to retire, play golf, collect seashells. Yet I was constantly on the go.

Busy--but strangely disconnected. Maybe the busyness was a way to keep from feeling, from revealing what my heart already knew.

The day before I left, I met with the person I had begun referring to as my "Last Supper." I wanted to see if there was anything left worth saving—just in case the problems were only my perspective. But our time together only confirmed what I already knew. Four years of struggle had brought us to this moment. It was time to move on and write the next chapter.

Despite this knowledge, when we said goodbye, my soul sank. It was not because of the goodbye itself, but because it reminded me of what I needed to leave behind—and how deeply that negative energy had drained me.

That night I called upon my guardian angel. What followed was one of the deepest conversations I've ever had.

I rarely cry. Years of emotional abuse in my past marriage had trained me to see tears as weakness, but during that conversation, something shifted. A single tear rolled down my face as I asked the question that had been echoing in my mind: "Why does it feel like everything is falling apart since I came back to Orlando when everything was going so well?"

The response came gently. "Sometimes things need to fall apart before they can actually fall into place."

I had heard that phrase many times before. Through spiritual teachers like Gabby Bernstein, the teachings behind *The Secret*, Jack Canfield, and many others. But this time, it landed differently. This time, it pierced straight through me.

Then came the next question. "What are you holding onto?"

I paused. What *was* I holding onto? Was it a person? A place? A past version of myself? Or was it something deeper—a fear-based mindset of scarcity that had been embedded in me since childhood despite all the personal growth work I had done?

My guardian angel continued. "When you realize what it is—and consciously choose to let it go—everything will begin to fall into place."

I laughed through the emotion. I said, "You remind me of the guy at the ashram in the movie *Eat Pray Love* who calls Julia Roberts 'Groceries.'"

But the humor couldn't hide what was happening internally. All of my teachings suddenly came rushing back like a tsunami. And one question remained: *What are you holding onto?*

The next morning, I packed my bags again. My next stop was Virginia, where I would spend time with friends and visit my son.

As the plane taxied down the runway and then lifted into the sky high above the clouds, the question stayed with me. What is it that I'm really holding onto? And more importantly . . . am I finally ready to let it go?

Chapter 13
TRAVEL LESSONS AND THE REALITY OF NOMAD LIFE

When people envision the nomadic life, they imagine that you close your front door, pick up a suitcase, and step into a world of effortless freedom—sunsets, spontaneity, lounging on the beach, eating fabulous food and meeting interesting people—adventure without responsibility. From the outside it looks simple and romantic.

But this version is a fantasy and it leaves out everything that makes it real. This life isn't just travel. It's logistics. It's planning. It's constant adjustment. It's learning how to create stability in a life designed to keep moving.

I learned that quickly. Without a permanent home, even the smallest routines become systems you have to build yourself. You have to think ahead. I created a kind of "home base" at a trusted friend's house, a place where I could store essentials, regroup between trips, and reset before heading out again.

Everything else, I figured out as I went. I remember sitting in a resort villa in Orlando, realizing I was about to head north—to Virginia and New York—and every sweater I owned was packed away in storage. Years of living in Florida had tricked me into thinking I didn't need them. So, there I was, ordering cold-weather clothes to arrive just in time for my next destination.

That's the rhythm of this life. You're either planning three steps ahead or solving the problem you didn't see coming. And the problems do come—usually in ways you don't expect. Like returning to your SUV after weeks away and discovering the key fob battery is dead. Or pulling into a resort at night and seeing your tire pressure light flick on. Small inconveniences in a normal life, but when you're constantly in motion, they require immediate attention.

In those moments, I found myself deeply grateful for one thing I had taken for granted before: a consistent business address. A place where everything could be sent, received, and managed no matter where I was. Without that, this lifestyle would unravel quickly.

Then came Europe—and with it, a whole new level of complexity. This wasn't just casual travel. There were cruises, formal nights, and appearances. Gowns, shoes, accessories—each one carefully considered, each one competing for space in a single 50-pound suitcase. Every item had to justify its place.

And of course, just when I thought I had it all handled, I realized I couldn't find my compression socks. Somewhere, packed neatly into one of my storage bins, they were completely out of reach. So I did what this life teaches you to do. I adapted. Overnight shipping became part of the plan. Because when you're constantly flying, constantly in transit, the small things—the things you might overlook in a stationary life—become essential.

The same was true for my health. I had to think months ahead, making sure I had enough of my natural hormone treatments to sustain me through long stretches of travel. There are no quick pharmacy runs when your next stop could be in another state—or another country.

And then there are the quieter questions. The ones that you don't even consider when you are at home and which aren't a big deal until you are on the road. Where do you do laundry? What pillow do you bring so you can actually sleep—and still stay under the airline weight limit?

How do you make a place feel like home when it isn't yours? For me, the answer was in small comforts. A scented battery-operated candle. A Firestick for the TV. Familiar routines I could recreate anywhere. Because no matter how beautiful the destination, you still need to feel grounded in it.

Even something as simple as food becomes more complicated. Eating out every day isn't sustainable—physically or financially—so I found myself navigating grocery stores in unfamiliar cities, piecing together meals, trying to maintain some sense of balance in a life that rarely stays still.

And then there are the financial realities. Freedom, as it turns out, is not free and requires discipline. Flights, accommodations, shipping, last-minute purchases—it all adds up. Managing that becomes part of the daily rhythm, whether you're aware of it or not.

Through it all, one thing remained constant. My laptop. It became my office, my connection to the world, my way of continuing to build something while I was moving through it. Writing, sharing, documenting—this journey wasn't just about seeing new places. It was about understanding them. Growing through them. Memorializing them. Becoming someone new within them.

There is something undeniably beautiful about living this way. When your life fits into a suitcase, you learn very quickly what you actually need—and what you don't. You stop holding onto excess. You begin to value time, connection, and experience over things.

But it's not effortless. There are sacrifices. There is discomfort. There are moments of exhaustion and doubt—times when you question whether it would be easier to just stay in one place and rebuild something familiar.

And yet . . . every time I faced one of those moments, I realized something: I could handle it. I could figure it out. I was more adaptable, more resilient, more capable than I had ever given myself credit for.

When you strip life down to its essentials—when you remove the layers of comfort and routine you once depended on—you come face to face with who you *really* are at your core.

And for me, that discovery has been the greatest journey of all.

Chapter 14

SIGNING UP FOR COURAGE

She didn't say it to hurt me. She said it simply—almost casually—in that way a close friend can speak candidly. "You're addicted to men . . . to being in a relationship."

There was a time I might have called it an addiction. But that word never quite fit. What I was really feeling—what I had always been feeling—was a deep, persistent desire to find my soulmate. A longing rooted in connection, in hope, in something profoundly human.

Another friend reframed this for me in a way that stayed. She said, "You're not broken—you're courageous. Maybe burnt out—but not broken." That distinction matters. Because burnout comes from trying, from caring, from showing up, again and again, despite disappointment. And courage is what keeps you open when it would be easier to close.

A different friend, someone who has spent years working with survivors of abuse, offered a perspective that shifted something even deeper. She reminded me that none of us sees the world the same way. We each move through life with our own set of lenses—shaped by our childhood, our experiences, our wounds, and our growth. Our blueprint is uniquely ours.

So who are we to judge how someone copes, what they seek, or how they love?

What one person labels as "too much" might simply be another person's way of reaching for connection in the only way they've learned. What looks like longing might actually be resilience. What feels like exhaustion might be the echo of hope that refuses to die.

I am not broken. I am someone who has felt deeply, tried fully, and learned continuously. And if that leaves me a little burnt out at times, it also means I have lived—and loved—with courage.

But what my friend at the top of this story couldn't see in that moment—and what I was only beginning to understand myself—was the pattern beneath my desire to connect. It didn't start in adulthood. It started much earlier, in a home where love wasn't always steady or expressed in the ways a child needs to feel secure. Especially from a father. There's something foundational about that relationship—something that quietly shapes how you see yourself, how you measure your worth, and what you come to expect from others.

When that need isn't met, it doesn't disappear. It follows you. It adapts. It hides. It finds new places to live.

You don't stop needing love—you just start looking for it in ways you don't always recognize. So no, I wasn't addicted to men. I was searching.

For validation.

For safety.

For reassurance.

For someone to reflect back to me what I hadn't fully learned to believe on my own—that I mattered, that I was enough, that I was worthy of being chosen fully and without condition.

And when that belief isn't rooted inside of you, you start outsourcing it. Quietly. Repeatedly. Different people. Same pattern. That realization didn't break me. It woke me up. For the first time, I wasn't looking outward for answers. I was willing to turn inward—to sit with what was uncomfortable, to question what I had always assumed was just "the way I am."

That's where courage actually begins. Not in the big, visible leaps people celebrate, but in the quiet decision to tell yourself the truth.

So, as I stepped into this season of my life—becoming a nomad, letting go of what was familiar, rebuilding from the ground up—I made a commitment to myself: I am signing up for courage. Not the kind that arrives all at once and changes everything overnight, but the kind that asks something of you, again and again.

Be honest.

Be accountable.

Be willing to see what you've been avoiding.

I started to shift how I moved through the world.

People were no longer there to complete me or validate me. Instead, they became mirrors—teachers reflecting back the parts of myself I still needed to understand.

Every interaction, whether easy or uncomfortable, held a question: Where am I still seeking approval? Where am I abandoning myself to be accepted? Where are the unhealed spaces still asking to be seen? Because those spaces—the quiet gaps we carry—don't disappear just because we ignore them. They show up in our choices. In our relationships. In the way we love, and in what we tolerate in return.

Courage is choosing to face them. Gently. Honestly. Without judgment.

And then choosing, even in small ways, to respond differently.

Now, each day, I ask myself a simple question: What is one thing I can do today that validates me? Not for anyone else. Not for approval or recognition. Just for me.

Some days, that means speaking my truth when it would be easier to stay quiet. Some days, it means setting a boundary and holding it. Some days, it means walking away from something—or someone—that doesn't meet me where I am. And some days, it looks like something far less visible: sitting in the discomfort of not being seen by others, while reminding myself that I still see me.

That's the work.

Because when you've spent a lifetime looking outward for validation, learning to give it to yourself can feel unfamiliar—almost unnatural at first. But it's also liberating in a way nothing else is.

I'm no longer waiting for someone else to choose me in order to feel worthy. I'm choosing myself. I'm no longer measuring my value by who stays. I'm defining it by how I show up for my own life. And in doing that, something powerful begins to shift. The pattern starts to break. Not all at once. Not perfectly. But intentionally.

Courage isn't about having everything figured out. It's about being willing to grow, even when growth feels uncomfortable. It's about choosing truth over illusion, again and again. It's about becoming the person you needed when you were younger—and offering yourself what you once searched for everywhere else.

So yes, maybe I was searching. But now I understand what I was *really* looking for. It was never a person. Never a relationship. Never something outside of me.

It was wholeness.

And that is something I am learning to build—slowly, deliberately—from the inside out. One courageous step at a time.

Chapter 15
RETURNING NORTH

Leaving Alexandria, Virginia, and then flying out of DCA felt like stepping across a threshold I had approached many times but never with quite this level of clarity. As the plane ascended, I carried with me a quiet awareness—an understanding that something unspoken had been gently tugging at me for years, waiting for acknowledgment. It wasn't fear or anxiety that stirred in my chest this time. It was honesty. Presence. A willingness to stop running from my past, and to stop avoiding. After all, those are the experiences that had shaped me.

After landing in Albany, New York, I moved through the airport with a kind of grounded anticipation. Picking up my rental car felt symbolic—my hands on the steering wheel, my body settling into the familiar ritual of driving north. The highway stretched ahead with familiarity, but internally the terrain was new, shifting. Childhood memories came not as precise images but as emotional fragments, waves that rose and fell with surprising gentleness. There was a time that I would have distracted myself, avoided them, but this time I didn't resist them. I simply let them come.

I had chosen Saratoga Springs intentionally. It was a beautiful city upstate with famous hot springs, Victorian charm, and an internationally renowned thoroughbred horseracing track, but I wasn't here to sightsee. It was close enough to see my father before continuing on to

Europe, yet far enough from my hometown to honor the emotional distance I still needed. It was as far as I could go without reopening doors I wasn't ready to walk through. My hometown sat just over an hour away, but that distance represented more than miles—it represented emotional territory I had not yet fully prepared to revisit. And that was okay. Today wasn't about forcing things that should not be forced.

My father still lives in a house in my hometown now, though not the one I grew up in. That alone felt symbolic: the past still exists, but not exactly where it once stood.

When I arrived, he greeted me with the same youthful spark he's always had, even at eightyfive. Time has etched its story across his face—lines deepened, posture softened, movements slowed—but his spirit moves with a kind of stubborn liveliness. He cracked a joke almost immediately, half shuffling, half strutting across the room.

"You know," he said with that familiar grin, "I can still outwork men half my age."

It made me smile, even as something inside me tightened. That's always been his way—jokes, stories, which could be conceived as distractions. A surface-level warmth that never quite dips into the deeper waters. And as he talked, mostly about my siblings and the grandkids, I felt that old sensation again: a strange invisibility, as if I were a supporting character in the room rather than his daughter.

But this time, something in me had shifted. I didn't look at him through the eyes of the child who longed for him, or the adult who spent years trying to make sense of his emotional absence. I saw him as a human being—shaped by his own unresolved history, raised in dysfunction he never learned to confront, carrying wounds he never acknowledged. He wasn't there for me in the ways I needed, and he'll likely never fully understand how that shaped me. At eighty-five, I no longer expect him to.

And from that place, I found forgiveness. It was not the kind that rewrites the past—it never does, nor can it—but the kind that releases me from holding it so tightly. Forgiveness is liberating.

I'll be with him over the next two days, choosing to enjoy the time we have. I'm grateful to see him in this season of life before his surgery, grateful for this brief overlap in our paths before I move on to the next stop in this nomadic chapter of my healing.

Later that evening, I shared pieces of my childhood with a friend who also grew up in our hometown. The conversation started casually—I mentioned that I was preparing to release my fourth book and then added, almost as an aside: "There's a lot you don't know about my upbringing."

She looked curious, then concerned, and as I explained a few of the more disturbing, graphic memories. Her expression shifted from casual interest to shock, disbelief. She had seen my family from the outside—put-together, functional, enviably "normal." That was the illusion everyone saw. The truth was that the fractures were always there, just hidden beneath the surface, like fault lines in the earth that sometimes shift and shake the foundations of our lives.

Giving voice to the incidents from my past wasn't about seeking sympathy. It was about acknowledgment—letting truth take its rightful place in the full landscape of my story. There was something freeing in letting another person see behind the curtain, even just a little.

Hearing her reaction reminded me just how powerful perception can be—and how easily truth can remain hidden behind a carefully constructed persona.

It was in that moment of reflection that I fully understood something important: many people live with versions of their lives that the outside world never truly sees. And for years, I had been one of them.

When I was driving north, I realized this trip had become something far more intentional than travel. My intuition, my guardian angels, my guides—if you will—had orchestrated the timing, the places, the conversations. Every step had aligned in a way that felt purposeful.

Saratoga Springs became my soft landing spot—an in-between space where I could pause, breathe, and honor my limits without abandoning my healing. I didn't need to drive farther north into the heart of my past to move forward. I simply needed to stand exactly where I was willing to stand.

And somewhere in that stillness, clarity settled. Peace with my father was never really about him. It was about me. It was about releasing the weight of old wounds so they wouldn't follow me into the next chapter of my life.

With that, the road ahead felt different—lighter, clearer, and entirely my own.

Chapter 16
THE GOODBYE THAT MATTERS

It was time. A quiet knowing settled in my chest as I prepared to say goodbye to my father. There was no dramatic moment, no big speech—just an awareness that this could be the last time I would see him. Age and life circumstances have a way of making you more honest with yourself. More present. More real. And I am a realist.

That truth didn't bring fear—it brought clarity. I was deeply grateful that I had made the trip.

What we shared during that time together was something I will carry with me forever. There were laughs that felt light and effortless, moments that reminded me of a simpler connection. We spent time at the casino, celebrating small wins like they were big ones, and time at the horse races, soaking in the energy, the excitement, the tradition of it all.

Simple moments. But the kind that becomes everything when you look at them in retrospect.

There was no need to overanalyze the past or force conversations that didn't need to happen. This wasn't about fixing anything. It was about *being*. About allowing space for joy, for presence, for appreciation of what *is* rather than what *was*.

And in that, I found peace.

As I said goodbye, I didn't feel the heaviness I once would have. There was no gnawing, unresolved tension pulling at me, no need for more. Just gratitude. Just a quiet sense of completion for this chapter as it exists today.

That, in itself, felt like healing.

Now it was time to continue the journey.

There were other family members to visit, one more moment to experience before heading back to Orlando for a few days. And then—Europe. Five weeks of exploration, reflection, and discovery waiting ahead.

On paper, it all sounded exciting. And it was. But beneath that excitement, there was still uncertainty. I had always had a home base. A place to return to. A place that grounded me, even in the midst of chaos. Now, I had chosen to pull up that anchor, and while nomadic life was beginning to settle in, my mind still tried to categorize it as a "vacation."

Maybe because that felt safer. Maybe because calling it a vacation implied an eventual return to something familiar.

But this was different. This was life now.

And for the first time in the past two days, something shifted in a way I didn't expect.

I didn't think about business.

I didn't think about the future.

I didn't strategize, plan, or try to control what was coming next.

I simply existed in the present—fully.

Each moment felt like a gift—unrushed, unfiltered, and unburdened by the constant need to "figure it all out." I allowed myself to experience time differently, not as something to manage, but as something to receive.

And in doing so, I realized how rare that had been in my life.

For so long, I had been in motion—building, achieving, surviving, pushing. Even in moments of rest, my mind was always somewhere else, already moving ahead.

But here, in this in-between space of goodbye and what's next, I found something I didn't even realize I had been missing: stillness. Not the absence of movement, but the presence of peace. The kind that comes when you stop trying to control every outcome and instead trust that each step is unfolding exactly as it should.

As I move forward—from family visits, to Orlando, to Europe—I carry that with me. Not just the memories of laughter, horse races, and casino wins. But the deeper understanding that life isn't meant to be rushed through or constantly solved. It's meant to be *lived*.

And sometimes, the most courageous thing you can do isn't planning the next move. It's allowing yourself to fully feel the one you're in before letting it go.

Chapter 17

CHOOSING FORGIVENESS, CHOOSING COURAGE

The trip to New York changed something in me.

It was not in a loud, dramatic way that announces its arrival—but in a quiet, undeniable shift that I could feel deep within my soul. Solid. Permanent. The kind of shift that doesn't demand attention but instead settles in and brings clarity. Peace. Understanding.

Psychologists talk about how trauma early in life settles deep into your mind and body. People often refer to it as "baggage" filled with the flotsam and jetsam collected over the years that you carry into everything you do. Relationships. Jobs. The way you react to adversity. For so long, I carried my childhood with me. Not always in ways I could see, but in ways I could feel viscerally deep in my bones.

The sounds.

The visions.

The moments that etched themselves into my memory before I even had the ability to process what they meant.

And the truth is, those things don't just disappear. They don't fade because you want them to or will them to. They don't erase themselves with time like rocks eroding in a river. They live in the body. In the subconscious. In the quiet spaces that resurface when you least expect it.

This trip didn't erase any of that. But it did give me something I didn't have before: perspective.

For the first time, I was able to look at my father not just as "Dad" but as a human being with his own story. His own pain. His own upbringing that shaped the man he became. I began to understand that he, too, came from something difficult—something that likely influenced the way he showed up in life, in relationships, and in parenting.

And my mother, too. There are still questions there. Still things I may never fully understand. But what I do know is this: No matter what someone has been through—no matter their pain, their past, or their circumstances—abuse is never the answer.

That truth stands firm.

And yet, alongside that truth, I've come to accept another: Parents raise their children the best they can with the tools they have at the time.

That doesn't make everything okay.

It doesn't excuse the pain.

But it creates space for understanding without abandoning accountability.

And somewhere between those two truths—I found forgiveness.

Not easily.

Not quickly.

And certainly not without resistance.

Forgiveness, for me, has not been a single moment. It has been a process. A choice I've had to make over and over again, especially when old memories resurface or when the emotional weight of the past digs into me and tries to pull me backward.

There were years of trauma. Years of carrying things I didn't have the tools to process at the time. Years of trying to make sense of experiences that shaped how I saw myself, how I trusted others, and how I moved through the world.

So, no—this hasn't been easy. But I've realized something that changed everything: Holding onto the pain doesn't protect me—it keeps me tied to it. And I don't want to live there anymore.

I want more for my life.

I want peace.

I want joy.

I want freedom.

And I want the ability to fully step into my dreams without being anchored to the weight of what I've already survived.

So, I made a choice. A conscious, courageous choice: to forgive.

Not because it was deserved.

Not because it was easy.

But because I deserve to move forward.

Because my dreams are bigger than my fears. Because the life I am creating requires space—space that cannot exist if it's filled with resentment, anger, or unresolved pain. And, most importantly, because courage is the cure.

Not the absence of fear.

Not the denial of what happened.

But the willingness to face it, feel it, and still choose to rise beyond it.

This chapter of my life isn't about forgetting. It's about freeing.

Freeing myself from the emotional chains of the past.

Freeing my future from being defined by what I've already lived through.

Freeing my heart to experience life in a new way.

With openness. With strength. With courage.

And for the first time, I can honestly say: I am no longer just surviving my story. I am choosing how it continues.

Chapter 18
THE WEIGHT OF LESS

As I prepared to pack up my things in New York—getting ready to head back to Orlando for a few days before embarking on my five-week journey through Europe—I found myself looking at my suitcase differently.

It was not just at what was inside the suitcase, but at what the suitcase and the contents represented. I laid everything out and took stock. What I had packed. What I had actually worn. What sat untouched, taking up space—space that suddenly felt heavier than it should have.

And in that moment, something clicked. There is more value in *less* than in *more*. It sounds simple. Almost cliché. But when you are living out of a suitcase—when every pound matters, when every item must earn its place—you begin to understand this truth in a much deeper way. It was about far more than exceeding the airline's weight limit.

My suitcase had been overpacked. Not just physically, but mentally, emotionally.

I had packed for a never-ending list of "what ifs."

What if I needed this?

What if it is raining?

What if it is snowing?

What if it is hot?

What if I have a special occasion?

What if my shoes aren't comfortable?

What if my shoes aren't dressy?

What if I wanted this option?

What if I wanted that option?

What if I didn't have enough?

That same mindset—the one rooted in fear, scarcity, and over-preparation—was the same one that once filled a 2,138-square-foot home and a two-car garage. The one that required dusting and sorting all that stuff in the big house. The one that made me forget and buy duplicates of things that I didn't need in the first place.

And now here I was . . . living out of a suitcase.

It made me pause and reflect on what I still had sitting in two storage units. Boxes filled with things I once believed were important. Necessary. Valuable.

But were they really?

As I began preparing for Europe, I made a decision: Everything I pack must be intentional.

When you are limited to a fifty-pound suitcase and a personal item, there is no room for excess. No space for indecision. Every piece must serve a purpose. It must fit well, feel good, wash easily, dry quickly, mix-and-match, and move with you—not weigh you down.

And in that realization, my entire perspective shifted. I would rather have a few high-quality pieces than an abundance of "just in case."

Yes, quality may cost more upfront—but it gives back in ways excess never can. Better fit. Better function. Better experience. And ultimately—less weight.

Less physical weight.

Less mental weight.

Less emotional weight.

And isn't that what we are all really searching for?

We live in a world where we have more than ever before, yet we are more stressed and disconnected than ever. We accumulate things—often from comparison, from trying to measure up, from filling spaces we don't quite understand.

We binge on the wrong things. Stuff. Noise. Distractions. All the while we are starved for what we truly crave: connection. We hold onto objects because of the memories attached to them, believing that letting go of the item means losing the moment. But the truth is—the memory isn't in the object. It's in us. Always has been.

As I prepare for Europe, I find myself reflecting not just on what I'm packing—but on what I've already let go of.

When I released the majority of my belongings, I didn't just create space for myself. I added value to others. Items that once sat unused in my life became meaningful in someone else's. What I no longer needed became something someone else appreciated, used, and valued. There is something deeply powerful in that exchange.

Letting go didn't take away from my life. It expanded it. Because in releasing "stuff," I made room for what truly matters.

People.

Connection.

Presence.

Time.

Time to sit with my thoughts.

Time to reflect deeply.

Time to evaluate what truly matters and what doesn't.

And in that space, something beautiful has emerged: growth.

Not rushed. Not forced. But intentional.

I've begun to build more meaningful relationships—ones rooted in presence, not convenience. Ones that are chosen with intention, not filled out of habit or fear of being alone.

This nomadic life, which once felt uncertain, is beginning to reveal its gifts. Not in what I have. But in what I no longer need.

As I zip up my suitcase—lighter, more thoughtful, more aligned—I realize this journey isn't just about traveling across countries. It's about traveling inward.

Releasing the excess.

Refining what matters.

And carrying only what truly adds value—not just to my life, but to who I am becoming.

Because in the end, the lighter we travel, the freer we live.

Chapter 19
THE FINAL GOODBYE

Leaving behind what no longer serves your highest good is rarely a single, dramatic moment that announces its arrival with great, unmistakable fanfare. It is a gradual unfolding—a series of quiet, deeply personal decisions. Some are painful. Some are empowering. All of them require honesty. And this trip, more than anything else, became about that process for me.

It became about the final goodbye.

As I returned to Orlando for five days, something within me shifted. Not in some loud or earth-shattering way, but in a calm, grounded knowing. The kind of knowing that no longer debates or negotiates. The kind that doesn't seek reassurance or explanations anymore. It simply arrives and says, *this is done.*

For the first time in a very long time, I wasn't replaying the past on a video loop in my head or clinging to what used to be. I was fully present with what *is*. I noticed what felt peaceful and what felt heavy. What nourished me and what drained me. What belonged in my life—and, more importantly, what no longer did.

There is a certain clarity that arrives only when you finally give yourself space. Your mind is not filled with clutter. Distance creates perspective. Silence creates truth.

As I sat with everything I had lived, everything I had learned, and everything I had held onto for far too long, one truth rose above all the rest:

You get what you feel.

I had watched *The Secret* more than twenty times over the years. I understood the concept intellectually: focus on what you want, align your thoughts, stay positive. But this time was different. This time, it wasn't something I understood only with my mind.

This time, I felt it in my body.

Because it isn't about thinking or wishing your way into a better life. It's about *feeling* your way into one. What you feel—what you embody emotionally, energetically, on a daily basis—is what you call back into your life. And for too long, I had been holding onto something that didn't feel good. It took up residence and cast shadows where no light could enter, where no good could grow.

A four-year relationship that quietly, consistently took more than it gave.

But they were also four years filled with lessons. With growth. With pain. With awareness. And eventually—with acceptance.

The truth I had avoided for so long finally became undeniable: It no longer served my highest good.

There comes a moment in every journey when you stop making excuses. When you stop justifying behavior. When you stop trying to fix someone. When you stop hoping they will eventually become who you need them to be. Instead of explaining things away, you simply remember.

You remember who showed up for you. You remember who stood by you in the moments that mattered. And, just as clearly, you remember who added to your storm when you were already drowning.

Once that realization settles in, everything changes. Because once you truly see it, you can never unsee it.

And with that clarity came one of the most powerful decisions I've ever made in my life: to walk away with grace—because how you exit one chapter is how you enter the next.

No more energy. No more explanations. No more bargaining with my own boundaries.

There's a quote that says, "*The greatest insult to a narcissist is to give them no energy and move on with your life.*" And that is exactly what I chose to do. Not from a place of anger. Not from a place of bitterness or revenge—but from self-respect.

Healing requires boundaries. Growth requires courage.

So, no—he doesn't get to know where I am. He doesn't get to know who I'm with or what I'm building or where I'm going next. He doesn't get access to this new chapter of my life.

That is a privilege that no longer belongs to him.

This is my journey. I am the CEO of my life.

And for the first time, I truly understand what that means. It means I choose who gets access to my energy. It means I protect my peace with intention. It means I no longer abandon myself just to keep someone else comfortable.

That pattern—the one rooted in my past, in my childhood, in my need to be seen, loved, and validated—that pattern ends here.The chain is breaking. And it's about time.

Of course, there's a part of me that wishes I had learned these lessons sooner. That I hadn't spent years trying to fix something that was never mine to fix. That I hadn't stayed as long as I did.

But growth doesn't obey our timelines. It arrives when we're ready.

And maybe—just maybe—I'm not late at all. Maybe I arrived exactly when I was meant to. Because standing here now, in this moment of release and clarity, I can finally see the truth:

Everything—even the pain—was guiding me here. To this decision. To this freedom. To this version of myself. The one who no longer settles. The one who chooses peace over chaos. The one who understands that letting go isn't loss—it's alignment.

And as I close this chapter, I don't feel emptiness. I feel space.

Space for something better. Something healthier. Something deeply aligned with who I am becoming. Because everything is always working out for our highest good . . . even when we can't see it yet.

Chapter 20
THE FOLLOWING

We get so caught up in the following.

The followers.

The likes.

The views.

The comments—but only the good ones.

Social media sounds like such an innocuous term. What might have started as a genuine way to connect with people—family in faraway places, old friends, new friends, people you thought you might never see again—can easily turn into an obsession. The constant pull to document every moment so the world can see where we are, what we're doing, who we are with, and who we're becoming. But only the good parts: the fun, the flashy, the beautiful.

And I almost did it.

I had planned to film *everything*—every destination, every experience, every step of this journey. I told myself it was part of the process, part of building, part of sharing.

But deep down . . . that's not what my soul wanted. What my soul wanted was presence.

I had waited so long for this chapter. I had sacrificed so much to get here. And the last thing I wanted was to experience it through the lens of a camera—detached, distracted, and performing for an audience.

This moment wasn't about the world. It was about me.

I didn't want to miss the signs—especially the subtle ones. The ones that don't scream for attention but quietly guide you when you slow down enough to listen. The ones you only recognize through stillness, through prayer, through silencing your mind.

Because the truth is, the only place you truly "possess" in this world is the one inside of you. Everything else could be gone tomorrow.

And so, I chose presence over posting videos. I chose stillness over sharing. I chose to live in the moment instead of capturing it.

When I landed in Paris, I didn't immediately pull out my phone and flip off airplane mode. I simply moved through the airport, grounded, aware . . . open.

And then it happened. As I stood at baggage claim, watching suitcases circle endlessly around the conveyor belt, one passed by that made me stop. It had a cover with a message printed on it that said:

"Live your life by a compass, not a clock."

It was a simple phrase, but it somehow felt divinely inspired, a sign, a confirmation directed straight to my soul.

A whisper from something greater than myself reminding me that I was *exactly where* I was supposed to be—and exactly *how* I was supposed to be.

Not rushed. Not scheduled. But guided.

The carousel of bags kept spinning, but I didn't mind the wait. It took a while for my luggage to arrive, but even that felt intentional. My domestic flight upgrade to first class had already eased the journey—no extra baggage fees, priority handling—and when my suitcase finally appeared, it felt like everything was flowing exactly as it should.

At the exit, my driver was waiting, holding an iPad with my name on it. Simple. Seamless. But life always adds its moments of unpredictability.

I needed to use the restroom before the 90-minute drive ahead, but my driver didn't speak English—only French. For a brief moment, I felt that familiar tension rise . . . the need to control, to figure it out, to manage every detail. *How would I manage this? I took French in school. Could I dig up enough from my memory to communicate?*

And then, just as quickly, support appeared. A man standing nearby spoke both languages and helped translate effortlessly. Surrender. Flow.

The driver then took my suitcase and gestured to escort me to the restroom level, offering to hold it while I went.

And there it was. That internal dialogue.

The old voice: *I've got this. I'll take my bag.* The protective instinct. The survival mindset. The version of me shaped by years of needing to be in control.

The New York voice: *Don't take your eyes off your bag.*

But then . . . a new voice.

Calm. Certain. Surrender.

I made a conscious decision in that moment to trust. To release control. To lean into the flow of this journey.

A new version of me was emerging. A New Dawn.

I handed over the suitcase. And guess what? Nothing bad happened. Everything felt lighter. Easier.

The drive to Versailles outside Paris was peaceful, almost meditative. And when I arrived at my hotel, I felt something deeper than comfort. I felt alignment.

I had chosen this property intentionally. Not just for the travel privileges I had earned over years in the industry. Not just for its location—nestled away from the intensity of central Paris—but for what it represented.

Value.

Self-worth.

Expansion.

This wasn't just a hotel stay. It was a reflection of how I was choosing to see myself now.

The walk to the magnificent palace of Louis XIV was misty, quiet, almost dreamlike. I found myself slowing down, breathing deeper, noticing everything—the air, the trees, the stillness. Nature has a way of bringing you back to yourself.

It wasn't just the surroundings that felt different, it was the people, too. Kinder. Warmer. More open. Or maybe—it was me. When you shift your energy, the world responds in kind. When you move through life with presence, gratitude, and openness, people feel it. And that energy has a way of returning to you in the most beautiful ways.

This chapter isn't about building a following. It's about following something far more important.

My intuition.

My peace.

My truth.

Because in the end, no amount of followers can replace the connection you build with yourself when you finally choose to be fully present in your own life.

And for the first time in a long time . . .

I am.

Chapter 21

THE RICHNESS OF FREEDOM

There is a richness to nomadic life that has nothing to do with money, status, or possessions. It isn't something you can measure or record or display. It's something you feel—quietly, deeply, in your body and in your breath. A fullness that doesn't come from accumulation, but from release.

When I first chose this path, I believed I was giving things up: stability, routine, a home base, the comfort of knowing exactly where I would be every day when I woke up. The next week, the next month, the next year. I thought I was stepping away from certainty. What I didn't realize was that in letting go, I was actually making space—space to breathe, space to feel, space to live with intention.

Nomadic life gently but insistently strips away the excess. Not just the physical clutter, but the emotional, mental, and spiritual weight we carry without realizing it. When you're no longer surrounded by familiar distractions, possessions, and routines, you come face-to-face with something far more confronting and far more honest: yourself.

At first, that can feel deeply unsettling. There's nowhere to hide. No busy calendar to distract you, no routines to pull you away, no noise loud enough to drown out your own thoughts, no familiar patterns to shield you from what's rising within. You are left alone with your consciousness, your inner world—and that silence can feel extremely uncomfortable before it feels liberating.

But then something beautiful begins to happen. You start to listen. To your intuition. To your body. To the quiet inner voice that has always been there, patiently waiting, buried beneath the weight of "more." Without the constant pull of obligations and expectations, you begin to hear yourself more clearly—and that clarity changes everything.

Nomadic life teaches you that freedom isn't found in having everything you want. It's found in learning how little you actually need. There is a lightness that comes when you realize you can live fully with a single suitcase, a handful of meaningful items, and an open heart. When you release the responsibility of maintaining a life filled with things, you suddenly become available for something else entirely: experiences, connection, and presence.

You begin to notice the world differently. The rhythm of birds awakening and singing in the early morning. The warmth of a stranger's smile in a country you've never been to before, communicating with no words spoken. The way a simple meal can feel like a luxury when you are truly present with it. Life slows down just enough for you to savor it.

You start to understand that richness is not defined by what you own, but by what you experience—and more importantly, by how deeply you allow yourself to experience it. Each moment becomes an invitation to be fully in the here and now.

When you free yourself from expectations, fear, and the need to control every outcome, you open the door to a different kind of life—one that flows rather than resists, one that surprises you, one that meets you in ways you never could have planned.

Freedom creates space for alignment. It allows the right people to find you, the right opportunities to unfold, the right moments to appear exactly when they're meant to. A quiet trust begins to develop—a knowing that you don't have to force everything, that life will meet you halfway if you allow it.

And perhaps the greatest gift of all is how your understanding of "home" begins to shift. Home is no longer a fixed place on a map. It becomes a feeling. Your cherished memories that live forever in your heart. A sense of peace you carry within yourself, no matter where you land. A groundedness that comes from being deeply connected to who you are.

That is the true richness of nomadic life. It's not about escaping. It's about returning—returning to yourself beneath the noise, the pressure, the expectations. Returning to a life that feels intentional, authentic, and free.

Because when you let go of what no longer serves you, you don't lose your life. You finally begin to live it.

Chapter 22

THE BEAUTY IN THE BECOMING

The day began in the most beautiful way—simply.

The morning started out slowly, leisurely, beautifully. I was not rushed. There was no need to be in a hurry because there was no schedule pressing in on me. There was no need to be anywhere other than exactly where I was. Over breakfast, enjoying a steaming cup of café au lait and a flaky, buttery croissant with blackberry preserves, I found myself lingering at the table longer than I might have at home, sharing conversation and easy laughter with new friends, Cathy and George from New Jersey. Cathy works with UNICEF, and there was something deeply grounding about connecting with people whose lives are rooted in purpose and service. Between the warmth of our exchange and the quiet attentiveness of the Waldorf hotel staff, the entire morning felt effortless—welcoming, human, unforced.

It reminded me how often the most meaningful moments arrive unexpectedly, slipping in when we finally slow down enough to notice them.

When I stepped outside, birdsong greeted me—not as background noise, but as something I truly heard. Something I felt. I walked slowly, aware of the rhythm of my steps and the steadiness of each breath. In that heightened awareness, a realization settled gently over me:

This is what life feels like when you are truly present.

The last twenty-four hours had been nothing short of extraordinary. Even the misty rain gently enveloping the trees and the ground and the people—once something I might have labeled an inconvenience—seemed infused with its own quiet magic. I smiled as I thought about the raincoat I'd found in Saratoga Springs, how a small and ordinary purchase had turned out to be perfect for this moment, this place, this season of life.

Everything felt aligned.

After settling into my room at the Waldorf, I took a quiet walk through the park. Nature has a way of guiding you back to yourself without effort or instruction. The stillness. The rhythm. The simplicity. In the distance, a horse grazed peacefully, entirely unbothered, fully immersed in its own existence. Watching it, I felt a soft but profound truth settle in me: life becomes incredibly rich when we allow ourselves to slow down.

Not rich in things. But rich in moments.

The birdsong.

The mist in the air.

The quiet that allows you to hear your own thoughts again.

These are the treasures we miss when we stay constantly plugged in, endlessly scrolling, always chasing something just beyond our reach. Beauty surrounds us every day—we simply forget to look.

Later, as I made my way to the Palace of Versailles, I was captivated not only by its grandeur, but by its artistry, its history, and the presence it carries. Walking those halls, surrounded by portraits that have watched centuries pass, I found myself drawn again and again to the women depicted in them. There was confidence in their posture, presence in their gaze, and a quiet, undeniable power that seemed to transcend time.

At least, that is what the paintings revealed.

Standing there, something stirred awake inside me—a reminder to return to my own power, to recognize my own value, and to stand fully in who I am without shrinking, questioning, or seeking permission. Those women became a mirror—not of who I once was, but of who I am becoming.

From Versailles, I continued on to the breathtaking, awe-inspiring splendor of the Notre Dame Cathedral, now refurbished after a devastating fire. Here, the energy shifted into something quieter and more reverent. It was Holy Week and Easter was just days away. With it came reminders of faith, renewal, and rebirth. It felt fitting. This entire journey has been about exactly that—shedding, healing, finding the light and beginning again.

On the way back to the hotel after a day of sightseeing, knowing I would soon be boarding a wine river cruise, I made a spontaneous stop at a small chocolate shop. The language barrier was real—our English and French equally imperfect—but presence did the work that words could not. The shopkeeper understood my nut allergy, my hesitation, and my curiosity. With patience and care, she guided me toward the most beautiful dark chocolate.

It was such a small moment. And yet, those are often the ones that stay with us the longest.

Connection does not require perfection. It requires presence.

Of course, I couldn't resist a stop for gelato—because when you're in Europe, you say yes to joy and delicious food.

Back at the hotel, I allowed myself a gentle reset. Room service arrived: beef bourguignon paired with a lovely French wine. Simple. Elegant. Nourishing. Later, I spent time by the pool, letting my body soften and my mind quiet in ways I hadn't realized it needed.

The day closed with an Aperol spritz at a restaurant inspired by Dave Ramsey—an unexpected but perfect ending. A blending of worlds, influences, and intentions that somehow made complete sense.

As I sat there, reflecting, one truth became unmistakably clear: everything in the last twenty-four hours had been a sign. Not loud or forceful, but steady and consistent. Gentle confirmations that I am on the right path. That my healing is unfolding exactly as it should. That by slowing down, disconnecting from the noise, and choosing presence over distraction, I am finally reconnecting with what matters most.

Myself.

I am completely in love with this experience—not because of where I am, but because of who I am becoming within it. And as I prepare for tomorrow, boarding my AMA Waterways wine river cruise—a dream I have carried for so long—I do so with a full heart, open eyes, and a deep sense of gratitude.

Because this is not just travel.

This is transformation.

Chapter 23
NAVIGATING THE JOURNEY

Travel isn't just about where you're going. It's about how you get there—and how smoothly everything flows along the way.

Over the years, I've learned that navigating travel well is both an art and a strategy. The difference between a stressful experience and a seamless one often comes down to a few key decisions made *before* you even leave your home.

In the Air

Let's start with airfare—because that's where every journey begins.

Scoring the best airline deals isn't about luck. It's about timing and awareness. In general, booking your flights about six to eight weeks in advance for domestic travel and two to four months ahead for international trips tends to yield the best pricing. Of course, there are exceptions, but waiting until the last minute rarely works in your favor unless you're incredibly flexible or just seeking an upgrade.

The day of the week you book is also important. Flying on or near the weekend is generally more expensive. The time of year can also impact the price. Flying in "shoulder season" usually in the spring (though not close to Easter) or fall can save you money. Plan to book even farther in advance if you are traveling in the summer or winter holidays.

Use search platforms like JustFly to explore pricing trends and compare options across airlines. These tools give you a strong snapshot of what's available in the market.

But here's the key—and it's one I stand by completely:

Always book direct.

Whether it's the airline or the hotel, booking directly with the company gives you better support if something goes wrong. Delays, cancellations, changes—when those moments happen (and they will), you want to be dealing directly with the source, not a third party.

The same goes for earning points and loyalty perks.

If you want the upgrades, the flexibility, and the recognition—you need to stay within the brand ecosystem. You can often transfer points from your credit card to an airline or hotel partner. Check for point boosters.

You can even take it a step further by signing up for airline and hotel credit cards that offer points, upgrades, and free stays. These can be incredibly valuable tools when used strategically. However, discipline is key—*always* pay off your balance as soon as you're finished spending to avoid interest charges that can quickly outweigh the benefits.

Home Away from Home

And that brings us to accommodations.

Choosing where to stay can feel overwhelming. There are endless options—hotels, boutique stays, short-term rentals, hostels. For many, particularly younger travelers, hostels are appealing due to price point, opportunities for socializing, and planned activities from cooking classes to guided tours. They absolutely serve a purpose for a segment of the tourist market.

But for me, after more than three decades working with resort brands, I value consistency and trust.

I tend to stay within brands like Hilton and Marriott—not just for the quality, but for the loyalty benefits that come with them. Late checkouts, room upgrades, points accumulation, and a certain level of service you can count on.

That said, even within these brands, there are tiers. A Hampton Inn will typically be more budget-friendly, while properties like Waldorf Astoria or Curio Collection offer a more elevated, luxury experience.

But here's something many travelers overlook: Not all hotels within a brand are created equal. Some are corporate-owned. Others are franchised. And that can impact everything from service to upkeep.

So, no matter how recognizable the brand name is—read the reviews. Always.

On the Ground

Now let's talk about transportation on the ground—because this is where your experience can either feel chaotic or completely effortless.

Private transfer companies are one of the best-kept secrets in travel.

Many people assume they are significantly more expensive than taxis—but that's not always the case. In fact, in many destinations, they are comparable in price and offer a far superior experience.

Pre-booked.

Professional drivers.

Clear communication.

No guessing, no negotiating, no fear of being taken advantage of in a foreign country, no stress after a long flight. Instead, you exit customs and find a smiling face holding a sign with your name on it.

During my time in France, I had an exceptional experience with a company called BT-Transfer. Seamless, reliable, and worth every euro.

But again—do your research.

Read reviews. Check ratings. Not all services are equal, and a little due diligence goes a long way.

When it comes to rideshare, it's also important to understand that not every country operates the same way.

In Portugal, for example, I found myself using Bolt instead of Uber. It was more widely available and often more cost-effective.

Each platform has its own policies, pricing models, and availability depending on where you are in the world—so take a moment to familiarize yourself with what works best in your destination.

Because the goal isn't just to get around. It's to move through your journey with ease—and that's really what all of this comes down to.

Engaging and Exploring

When it comes to truly experiencing a destination, booking excursions can elevate your trip from simply visiting a place to actually *connecting* with it. I personally love using Airbnb Experiences because they offer smaller, more intimate group settings and a level of detail you don't always get with larger tour operators. There's something special about being guided by locals who are passionate about what they do—it creates a more personal and memorable experience. From a vintage car tour through the streets of Rome, to a rock-and-roll tour in London, to a beautiful boat experience along the coast of Portugal, these moments became highlights of my journey. They weren't just excursions—they were stories, connections, and they formed memories that I'll carry with me long after the trip ends.

Travel doesn't have to be complicated, but it does require intention.

When you plan your flights wisely, choose accommodations you trust, book directly for support and benefits, leverage credit wisely for rewards, and select transportation that prioritizes your experience—you create a foundation that allows everything else to unfold beautifully.

Because when the logistics are handled, you're free to be present—to experience, to savor, to learn, to connect, to be spontaneous and take advantage of serendipitous moments minus the stress. And that's where the real magic of travel begins.

Chapter 24
A DREAM ALONG THE SEINE

There are moments in life when everything aligns so beautifully, so effortlessly, that you can't help but pause and think: *This is what it's all about.*

My time in Normandy and Paris aboard the AmaWaterways wine cruise was exactly that. It was a dream realized.

From the moment I stepped into my cabin, I knew this experience would be different. Thoughtful. Intentional. Elevated in a way that went beyond luxury—it felt personal. A beautiful gift scarf awaited me, delicately placed as a colorful and elegant welcome. Later, a chocolate bunny appeared on my pillow, a small but meaningful touch that made me smile.

It wasn't just about what was provided to me as a guest—it was about how it made me feel.

Seen. Considered. Cared for.

The staff carried that same energy throughout the entire journey. Their smiles were genuine, their organization seamless, and their attention to detail unmatched. Every movement, every interaction, every transition from one experience to the next felt effortless—as if they had anticipated your needs before you even realized them yourself.

I have food allergies—so it's not just a matter of likes and dislikes for me. The level of care means everything to me because my health is at risk. Every meal was handled with precision and thoughtfulness. There was never a moment when I hesitated, thought twice before I took a bite, or became concerned. Instead, I was confident. The kind, professional and caring staff gave me reassurance that I could fully relax and enjoy the experience without worry that I might have an adverse reaction.

That kind of attention allows you to truly *be present*. To savor not just the food—but the moment.

Of course, the destinations themselves were breathtaking. Normandy, rich with history and depth. Paris, timeless and alive with culture. Experiencing these places is always special—but what elevated the experiences even further were the local guides.

They didn't just share information. They told stories. They brought history to life in a way that made you feel connected—to the people, to the culture, to the land, to the moments that shaped it. Their passion was contagious, and it transformed each excursion into something far more meaningful than a simple tour.

It became an experience.

Onboard, the journey continued in the most unexpected and beautiful ways.

We were joined by a winery from Washington state, with presenters Brian and Brandee leading the experience. And while the wine itself was exceptional—the pairings, the selections, the knowledge—it was who they were as people that truly stood out.

Their humility.

Their warmth.

Their genuine connection with others.

They didn't just represent a brand—they embodied it.

It wasn't about selling wine. It was about building relationships.

You could feel it in every interaction, every conversation, every shared moment. They created an atmosphere where people felt welcomed, included, and valued—whether you were a long-time club member or meeting them for the first time. That kind of authenticity is rare—and it leaves a lasting impression.

But perhaps the most meaningful part of the entire journey wasn't the destinations, the food, or even the wine. It was the people.

Traveling solo often comes with its own set of emotions. There's freedom, of course, and no waiting on others, negotiating where to visit or where to eat, but there can also be moments of solitude that some might find lonely. Moments where you're reminded that you're experiencing it all on your own.

But not on this trip. From the very beginning, connections formed naturally, and before long, I found myself surrounded by people who no longer felt like strangers—but like family. Al. Lynn. Jan. Names that will forever be tied to laughter, shared meals, meaningful conversations, and moments that made this journey unforgettable. We connected in a way that felt easy. Genuine. Effortless.

And in doing so, they gave me something I didn't even realize I needed: A sense of belonging. They made me forget that I was traveling alone—because I wasn't. Not really.

That's the magic of experiences like this. They remind you that connection can happen anywhere. That family isn't always defined by blood—but by the people who show up, who share space with you, who make you feel seen and valued exactly as you are.

As the journey came to a close, I found myself reflecting on everything it had given me.

Not just memories—but meaning.

Not just moments—but connections.

Not just a trip—but a reminder of what life can feel like when everything aligns.

This wasn't just a wine cruise. It was an experience of the heart. And one I will carry with me—long after the river has passed.

Chapter 25
EXPECT THE UNEXPECTED

If there's one thing travel will teach you—again and again—it's this: You can research, get advice from all the experts, go through a travel agent, plan everything down to the last detail . . . and still need to pivot. Like death and taxes, changing course is inevitable.

No matter how organized you are, how many years of experience you have, or how carefully you map out your journey, travel will test you. Delays, changes, missed connections, miscommunications, unexpected costs—it comes with the territory.

And the difference between stress and flow? Preparation, and your ability to think on your feet—the latter of which gets easier with experience, which in turn builds confidence that you can handle whatever comes your way next time.

I was reminded of that in a very real way during a travel day that started less than ideal.

I had taken a day of rest at the Hilton Paris Charles de Gaulle Airport. I needed a day of rest because I had been on a river cruise, which was amazing but jam-packed with excursions and activities. Now. we weren't obligated to do them, but when everything is included you want to take it all in. I did skip out on one afternoon excursion because I was exhausted, so on paper, a day of rest sounded like exactly what I needed. In reality, I got little rest at all.

I slept only two hours and woke up feeling completely off—run down, foggy, and not at my best. I felt like I was coming down with something and my bronchitis had kicked in full force, so between not feeling well, unfamiliar surroundings, and needing to be up very early the next day, my brain just wouldn't turn off.

But travel doesn't pause for how you feel. So, I moved forward.

The hotel had arranged a taxi for me, but when the ride was complete, the fare came in higher than quoted. The cab driver was nice, and not trying to take advantage, and he even tried calling the hotel. It was so early, however, apparently only one staff member was on duty and didn't pick up. Rather than wait for a callback, I said, "I have to go, I have to catch my flight." So instead of 25 Euros he quoted me, I negotiated with the driver, calmly and confidently. I handed him 20 Euros—cash—and said I would take it up with the hotel. He said that was okay.

A reminder in real time: *Always* carry local currency. Credit cards are convenient, yes—but cash still holds power. It gives you flexibility, leverage, and options when things don't go as planned. As we say in the States: Cash is king.

Arriving at the airport, there were no upgrades available. My suitcase? Over the weight limit. Another hurdle that would cost me money—75 Euros!

But instead of frustration or whipping out my credit card, I shifted into solution mode.

The airline agent offered me the option to reposition items from my luggage into my carry-on. Not ideal, but workable. And that's the mindset—*work with what's in front of you.*

Early morning flights aren't exactly known for abundance of food and shopping, and this one proved it. Options were limited at the gate. A small win—there was a Starbucks. No breakfast sandwiches, but coffee would have to do.

And thanks to a nearby shop, I managed to grab what the English call a bag of crisps, known in the United States as chips.

Not glamorous and definitely not healthy—but it was enough to keep my hunger at bay until I could get better food.

Boarding the flight, everything seemed normal at first. Passengers seated, ready for departure. But something felt off. The cockpit door remained open longer than usual. Then it closed and we pushed back. And then—noises. Unusual ones. Moments later, the engine shut down. The captain came on to explain there was an issue with a passenger door sensor that required repair. So there we sat. On the tarmac. Waiting. An hour passed. And here's the thing most people don't consider—it's not just about fixing the issue. Once resolved, there's still coordination required for takeoff clearance, scheduling, and arrival sequencing, especially into a busy airport like Heathrow.

Time was slipping. My connection was at risk since I only had an hour between my two flights, which we had burned through sitting on the tarmac. Concerned, I turned to the flight attendant and asked about my connecting flight.

"Let's wait and see," she said.

But I knew better. After thirty-four years in the travel industry, I've learned one critical lesson: Don't wait and hope things will work out.

When delays happen and connections are tight, you have to act *immediately*. Because you're not the only one affected—there are dozens of passengers trying to rebook at the same time. So, sitting right there on the tarmac, I called British Airways. Hold. International delay. Disconnected. I tried again. Switched to the chatbot. Glitch. Reset.

By the time I made progress—it was time for takeoff.

At that point, I had to surrender the outcome—but not the effort. In the air, I attempted to connect to Wi-Fi. Nothing. No access. No updates. Just uncertainty.

And sometimes, that's part of the journey too.

But the moment we landed at Heathrow Airport, everything shifted. My phone reconnected.

And there it was. A notification. My flight had been canceled—and I had been automatically rebooked on the next available flight to Faro!

Not the seat I originally chose—window instead of aisle—but it didn't matter. I had a seat. I had a path forward.

Making my way through the airport, I passed a long line at the help desk—and then something unexpected happened. A British Airways attendant stood nearby, holding a ticket. "For Dawn, to Faro."

Seamless. Aligned. Handled. Still, I continued to the central desk to confirm everything—and that's when I met Satnam.

Out of multiple agents, I found myself drawn to him. I had watched him assist other passengers—one in a wheelchair, another navigating a complex situation—with patience, kindness, and genuine care.

And quietly, I hoped I would be next. Moments later, I was. Satnam not only confirmed my rebooking, but he elevated it with an upgrade to Business Class—what they call First Class in the U.S.

Just like that, the entire experience shifted. From stress . . . to ease. From uncertainty . . . to gratitude.

I made my way to the lounge, finally able to sit, breathe, and eat something substantial. Then back to the gate—with a quick stop at the Harrods shop for a makeup bag. Because sometimes, it's the little resets that help you feel like yourself again.

Boarding the flight, the energy was completely different. The service. The space. The calm.

And when we landed in Faro—my suitcase was there waiting. Seamless. Again.

Through customs I went, and then—there she was: Lorraine, my friend of 36 years.

And in that moment, none of the delays, the stress, or the uncertainty mattered anymore. I had arrived. And I was exactly where I was meant to be.

That's the thing about travel. It will test you—but it will also reward you.

And if you stay prepared, stay flexible, and trust your ability to navigate the unexpected, you'll find that even the most challenging moments have a way of working out.

Sometimes even *better* than planned!

Chapter 26
RUNNING ON EMPTY, LIVING FULLY

There's a certain kind of truth that only shows up when you're exhausted. When your body is running on two hours of sleep. When your mind is foggy and you feel like you are walking through thick mud with heavy shoes. When you have nothing left to give physically, mentally, emotionally, and yet somehow, life still asks you to show up. So you do.

Arriving at the Hilton Vilamoura, I thought I knew what to expect. I had been there before. Vilamoura is a beautiful golfers' paradise. It is popular with Irish and Brits who go there for the sunny weather, and nice beaches. It has a tropical feel, and the Conrad is about 20 minutes away in Quinta do Lago, which is called "Millionaires Row" because of the posh surroundings.

I remembered the warmth at the Hilton. The familiarity. The staff who made you feel like you mattered—not just another guest, but someone they genuinely cared about. But this time, something felt different. I looked forward to seeing familiar, friendly faces, but they were gone.

In their place was a more corporate energy. Polished, efficient—but missing that warmth I had once loved so much. The staff were polite and smiled, but their intent didn't quite reach the same heartfelt depth. While I understood, of course, that everyone was doing this work to make a living to support themselves and their families, the experience nevertheless felt transactional.

It was a quiet reminder that nothing stays the same. Not places. Not people. Not even the things we once held onto for comfort.

And yet—there was still something to be grateful for. My room had been upgraded, overlooking the pool. It came with a beautiful view, peaceful and calming. And more importantly, I was finally reunited with Lorraine.

Thirty-six years of friendship. The kind of connection that doesn't need effort—it just *is*.

I originally met Lorraine when I was twenty-two. A year later, she came to stay with me in Orlando, in the home from my first marriage, when she was on holiday. When I was in the Jersey Channel Islands at twenty-three, on holiday, I wanted to look her up, but I didn't have her number, so I scoured the phone book—yes, people back then used them—and called seven people with her last name. Nobody who answered knew her, and I had given up trying to see her. The next morning, I got a pleasant surprise when there was a knock on my hotel room door. There was Lorraine with a dozen red roses. She said, "Right, pack up your stuff, you are coming to stay with me."

As often happens when you get busy with life's responsibilities, I lost track of her for 31 years but I posted two years ago on Facebook that I was going to Vilamoura. She messaged me that she lived close by, and we had a wonderful reunion and haven't lost touch since.

On this trip, we could have talked for hours. And in many ways, it felt like we already had. But time had been stolen from us earlier in the day with delays and disruptions, so there was a sense of urgency now.

I quickly unpacked. Showered. Reset. There was no time to linger. It was already late, and dinner hours had passed. But when you're with someone who matters, the timing doesn't matter nearly as much as the moment.

So we headed out to Lorraine's favorite Irish pub. Even though I was running on fumes, I came alive. There's something powerful about being in the presence of people who energize you. The laughter, the music, the familiarity—it fills you in a way sleep sometimes can't.

We sang.

We laughed.

We people-watched like it was our favorite pastime.

And for the first time in a long time, we were just . . . *there.*

Not distracted.

Not rushed.

Not divided by life's responsibilities.

Just two friends, fully present, soaking in the joy of being together.

Time slipped away. Before we knew it, it was 1:30 AM. I don't know how I made it that long—but I did. I made it back to the room at 2 AM, knowing full well that my alarm was set for 7:45 AM. The plan? Shower, reset, and be ready for our 9:30 brunch. Why so early? We had planned for a full day. Brunch is served until 11 AM and we had to pack in laundry plus meet a friend of Lorraine's at her house.

And somehow, I did it. That's the thing about travel—and life, really. You're capable of more than you think you are when your heart is full.

I made my way down to breakfast, cappuccino in hand, savoring that first moment of stillness. And then—just like old times—Lorraine arrived and filled the room with her magical aura. She effortlessly connected with everyone around her, captivating the dining staff with her energy and warmth.

We picked up right where we left off. Mimosas in hand. Laughter flowing in waves of joy. Stories unfolding and blossoming in the telling of them. It felt like no time had passed at all.

From there, the day continued in the most beautifully unexpected way. Laundry—because after two weeks of travel and three more to go, it was a necessity. Then meeting Lorraine's friend. Then there was a bikers' event followed by a tractor and music festival later that day—with the same rock band from the night before.

It was layered.

Unplanned.

Perfect.

And in the middle of it all, something became undeniably clear: What I already knew about Portugal was being confirmed once again.

The people are warm.

They are welcoming.

They live simply—not driven by materialism but by connection.

They find joy in being together. And that's what makes this place so special.

I made new friends.

Shared conversations.

I felt included.

Not because of who I am, where I've been, or what I've done—but simply because I was there, open, present, and willing to connect.

And that's when it hit me: These are the treasures.

Not the hotels.

Not the status.

Not the things we accumulate.

But the moments. The people. The connection.

We spend so much of our lives chasing meaning—looking for it in achievements, possessions, titles, and validation from the outside world.

I've done it too. But what the great teachers and gurus really mean when they say "everything you need is within you" isn't about isolation.

It's about *alignment*.

It's about becoming so grounded in who you are—so connected to your own light—that you naturally connect with others. That you enhance lives simply by being present.

By being real.

By being open.

Because at the end of the day, it doesn't matter: Who you are. Where you've come from. What you own. What you've achieved. What car you drive. How much money is in your bank account.

None of that defines the richness of your life.

What matters is this: Are you a joyful soul from the inside out? Can you connect?

Can you be present with others in a way that lifts, inspires, and unites? Because that's why we're here.

Not for the things.

Not for the status.

Not for the applause.

But to connect.

To uplift.

To enhance.

Running on empty, I found myself fuller than ever. And that's the kind of paradox only life—and travel—can teach you.

Chapter 27
SAY YES TO ME

I have learned that there is one non-negotiable that always takes precedence, whether you are at home or on the road: your health and well-being—especially when you are on the road. There comes a moment in every journey when your body speaks louder than all of your carefully curated plans.

And if you're wise—you listen.

After a nonstop river cruise schedule, a flight cancellation and rebooking, two hours of fitful sleep, and a beautifully chaotic twenty-four hours with Lorraine, I could feel it.

The subtle shift.

The quiet exhaustion.

The whisper of my body saying, *enough . . . for now.*

Travel has a way of testing your limits. It fills your soul, yes, but it can also deplete your system if you don't pause long enough to replenish. So, on this day, I made a decision.

I chose me. I said yes to my mind, my body, and my spirit.

Arriving at the Conrad Algarve, I immediately felt the shift. This wasn't just another stop on the journey—this was a sanctuary.

From the moment I stepped onto the property, I was greeted by impeccable service. Warm smiles. Polished uniforms. A level of attentiveness that instantly made me feel seen, welcomed, and valued.

I was offered a chilled, refreshing glass of water. A luxurious, cool towel was placed gently in my hands, and I felt renewed. Just like that, the outside world melted away.

If there is ever a place to feel truly pampered, this is it.

Lush, manicured grounds. Exquisite design. Rooms that feel less like accommodations and more like an experience. I knew immediately—this would be my retreat. An oasis. A place to pause, to breathe, to reconnect.

Vítor graciously provided a private tour of the Infinity Penthouse Suite—complete with its own private garage—something I would later feature on my travel platform. The level of detail, the architecture, the thought behind every element . . . it was inspiring. (thriveandtravel.com)

And then, as if perfectly timed, my room was ready—with an upgrade. I had:

A beautiful balcony overlooking the pool.

A chilled bottle of champagne welcoming me back after two years. Traditional Portuguese pastries (*pastéis de nata*) delicately placed, inviting me to indulge.

Even the smallest details were considered—a fully stocked fridge with both still and sparkling water (or as they say here, water "with gas"), complimentary and thoughtfully arranged.

Everything exceeded my expectations. And more importantly—it made me feel worthy of it.

By the time I unpacked, the afternoon was slipping away. I made my way down to The Nest, the hotel's lounge, and ordered something I wouldn't normally choose—a cucumber mint martini; the welcome drink compliments of the Conrad Algarve.

It tastes as good as it sounds. Refreshing. Light. Unexpected. And absolutely perfect.

It was past lunch and too early for dinner, but I needed something to eat so I opted for something simple. A seafaring country, Portugal is known for its cod, and I had yet to experience it on this trip, so I ordered the cod dip. It did not disappoint. It was bright, fresh, flavorful, and amazing.

But even after that moment of pause, I realized something: I still hadn't truly *rested.* Back in my room, I lay on the bed—soft, inviting, almost cloud-like—and my mind wandered to the spa. The pool. The sauna. The steam room. The heated stone beds. The hydrotherapy pool with its soothing jets. All included. All waiting. Why not for me?

But what my body truly craved was deeper. A massage. And almost immediately, the old shaming pattern surfaced.

Do you really need that?

You could spend that money elsewhere.

It's not necessary.

That voice—the one that shrinks. The one that says *no* to yourself. But this time was different. This time, I caught it—and I answered it before it could try to reason with me.

Not today.

I made a quiet agreement with myself: *If it's meant to be, they'll have availability.* Now, realistically, at a fully booked luxury hotel with the spa closing in just a few hours, the odds weren't in my favor. But I called anyway.

And just like that: "Yes, can you be here in 10 minutes?"

I smiled. "Absolutely!"

Because sometimes, saying yes to yourself opens doors you didn't expect.

I made my way down, where Madelena was waiting. Calm. Professional. Grounded. She guided me through the experience with ease—locker, plush robe, quiet transitions—and before I knew it, I was lying in the treatment room, ready for a sixty-minute reflexology session.

Many think that reflexology is a fancy term for a foot massage. It's actually something much more complex. It's a specialized, holistic, non-invasive therapy that works through mapped pressure points in the feet, hands, or ears—each one corresponding to specific organs and systems in the body.

Where traditional massage focuses on muscles, reflexology works with energy, circulation, and internal balance.

It is subtle but powerful, and it can support:

- Detoxification
- Improved circulation
- Reduced stress and anxiety
- Enhanced sleep quality
- Immune system support
- Hormonal balance
- And overall restoration of the body's natural equilibrium

Not everyone knows how to do it well. But Madelena was a master. Within minutes, my body softened. My breath slowed. And somewhere between awareness and surrender—I drifted. A light sleep. Even a soft snore, I later realized. And for the first time in what felt like weeks . . . my body let go.

Time passed too quickly. I didn't want it to end. But when it did—I felt different.

Lighter.

Clearer.

Renewed.

It was as if the past month and a half of constant movement, stimulation, and stress had simply . . . dissolved. And in that moment, a realization settled in:

You deserve this. Not someday. Not when everything is perfect. Not when you've "earned it." Now.

I took a few quiet moments afterward, capturing the stillness of the spa as it neared closing. I lay on the heated stone bed, letting the warmth sink in, grounding me.

I was grateful. Deeply grateful.

Tonight wasn't about going out. It wasn't about meeting new people. It wasn't about finding the next undiscovered local restaurant or chasing the next experience. It was about me.

Time alone.

Time to reflect.

Time to write.

Time to honor the journey I had waited so long to begin.

Because in a world that constantly pulls us outward, that constantly tries to bargain with us, or tells us why we should say no, there is something incredibly powerful about turning inward and saying *yes.*

Yes to rest.

Yes to healing.

Yes to worth.

Yes to yourself.

And in that yes—everything changes.

Chapter 28
THE CONVERSATION WITHIN

It's amazing how we can move through life carrying a quiet, often relentless, negative dialogue in our minds. It might go something like this:

I'm not thin enough.

I'm not fit enough.

I'm not pretty enough.

And then, years later, we look back at photos and think, *Wow . . . if I thought I was "that" then, what does that make me now a few decades, a few inches, and several pounds later?*

The irony is cruel. Because the truth is, it was never about the body. It was about the story. The story we make up about ourselves built on years of experiences that slowly kill the soul and eat away at our self-esteem.

That internal dialogue—the one that criticizes, compares, and chips away at our sense of worth—doesn't just appear overnight. It's shaped over time. It is built on the foundation of moments in childhood, experiences, environments, expectations. They compound and quietly form a blueprint long before we even have the awareness to question it.

It's a shrinkage mindset—making ourselves smaller in a world that already asks so much of us. We would never say these things to someone else, but we torment ourselves without a second thought.

But here's the reality no one talks about enough:

There will always be someone thinner.

There will always be someone fitter.

There will always be someone younger.

There will always be someone perceived as more beautiful.

And on the flip side, there will always be someone wishing they were exactly where you are.

So where does that leave us? For me, this nomadic journey has become less about the places and learning new things and more about the *unlearning*. The rewiring. The conscious decision to interrupt that old narrative and replace it with something rooted in truth.

Because the truth is this:

I am turning fifty-seven.

I am living out of a suitcase.

I have endured years of crushing stress.

I have suffered four bouts of COVID.

I have lived with terrible hormonal imbalances.

I am living in a body that has carried more than most people will ever see on the surface.

Research shows that COVID can directly impact fat tissue, triggering inflammation and affecting metabolic health. Add years of stress to that, and the body doesn't just "bounce back" overnight. It takes time. Real time. Intentional time. Healing time.

And for the first time in my life, I'm allowing that to be okay.

Today, I was standing there, looking out at the beautiful pool at the Conrad Algarve, my new swimsuit from Versailles in hand. There was a moment—a pause—where the old voice tried to creep in.

Not yet.

Not ready.

Maybe when you lose a little weight . . .

But something inside me shifted. Because this journey isn't about waiting to arrive at some perfect version of myself before I start living. It's about accepting where I am. Honoring how I got here. And choosing, right now, to step into the life I've worked so hard to create.

I silenced the voices. I wore the swimsuit.

Not because everything was perfect—but because I am no longer willing to sit on the sidelines of my own life. One thing I know for certain: Your internal light will always outshine anything external.

And that's what so many people are searching for: not perfection, not validation, but that light. That energy. That presence that comes from within.

And for the first time in a long time, heading out to the pool, I feel it again. My joy.

Not because everything is flawless, but because I've reclaimed it. Protected it. Chosen it.

And I've made a promise to myself: Never again will I allow anyone—or anything, including those old voices from the past—to dim that light. Because I am the CEO of my own life.

And boundaries? They are everything.

Chapter 29
THE RICHNESS OF BEING

Wow, what a whirlwind it has been since returning to Vilamoura, Portugal, a coastal resort town in the Algarve region

There's something special about coming back to a place—not as a visitor rushing through, but as someone who can simply *arrive*—that shifts everything. This time, it wasn't about checking into a hotel or chasing the next story. It was about reconnecting, rediscovering, and allowing life to unfold naturally.

Reuniting with my beautiful friend Lorraine felt effortless, like no time had passed at all. Days melted into each other in the best possible way—poolside conversations under the sun, contagious laughter echoing between sips of cocktails, and slow, indulgent brunches filled with mimosas and stories that only deepen with time. There was no rush, no pressure—just presence.

We wandered through shops without purpose, not searching for anything specific, yet somehow finding exactly what we needed in the experience itself. It wasn't about what we bought, but about the shared glances, the spontaneous moments, and the quiet understanding that these are the memories that linger far longer than any material thing we could buy.

Then came the unexpected magic—meeting Aun from the DMV area. What began as simple curiosity about the rooster, Portugal's iconic symbol, turned into something much more meaningful. Our conversation unfolded effortlessly, we shared stories that built on each other's stories, and in what felt like a fleeting moment, a new connection was formed—one of those rare encounters that remind you how small and beautifully connected the world really is.

And woven into these days were the new friends from Ireland I had met in the previous nights—connections that didn't end when the evening did but carried into the days that followed. Each of them brought their own stories, laughter, and perspective, adding another layer to this ever-evolving experience. There's something special about those kinds of encounters—when people enter your life unexpectedly and leave a lasting impression in such a short time.

These are the moments that stay with you. Because this is the richness of nomadic life.

It's not always about the destinations or the perfectly curated experiences. It's not about having somewhere to be or something to prove. In fact, it's the complete opposite. It's about having nowhere you *have* to be. No timeline dictating your next move. No rigid agenda pulling you in a certain direction. No expectations weighing on your shoulders.

And for once, no story you feel obligated to capture or share. Just . . . being.

And in that space—when you release the need to do, to plan, to achieve—you begin to notice something extraordinary. Life becomes fuller. Conversations become deeper. Laughter becomes louder. Connections become more meaningful.

You realize that the true luxury isn't the destination, the hotel, or the experience.

It's the people.

It's the poolside moment that becomes a memory you'll carry forever.

It's the stranger who becomes a friend within a single conversation.

It's the feeling of belonging without needing to stay.

In those moments, you discover something profound: the true meaning of life isn't found in what you accomplish or where you go next—it's found in the connections you make along the way.

And as the days in Vilamoura continue to unfold, one thing becomes clear . . .

These stories, these people, these moments—they don't just pass through your life. They become part of you.

Forever.

Chapter 30

FULL CIRCLE AT THE CONRAD

There are places in the world that welcome you. And then there are places that receive you. Places that pull you back in with a warm, loving embrace, and let you know that you are in the right place at the perfect time.

Returning to the Conrad Algarve felt like coming home—not in the traditional sense, but in that deeper, more meaningful way, where everything just feels *right*. From the moment I stepped back onto the property, there was a familiarity, a warmth, an unspoken understanding that this wasn't just another stay. This was a return to something that had already become part of me. It was like a déjà vu.

The staff has a way of making you feel like you belong, like you're not just passing through, but truly part of something. It's that rare "home away from home" feeling that so many places try to create, yet so few actually achieve.

João escorted me to my room, and what began as a simple walk quickly turned into something more. We spoke about life—not in passing, but in a way that felt grounded and real. The kind of conversation that only happens when both people are present.

We talked about quality of life. About the question so many of us wrestle with: Are we living to work, or working to live? And more importantly, if we do the latter, at what cost?

Yes, we can chase higher status. Yes, we can earn more money. But somewhere along the way, many lose the very thing they were chasing it all for—peace, joy, presence.

There was something powerful in that moment, standing in a place defined by luxury, yet discussing the simplicity that truly fulfills us.

Because the truth is, when we simplify our lives—when we strip away the noise and return to what really matters—something shifts. There's a natural joy that rises from within. A sense of fullness that no title, no paycheck, no external validation can replicate.

And as I've moved through life, accumulating wisdom through hard-earned experience, especially now in my fifties, that clarity has only deepened.

What once felt important no longer holds the same weight. The urgency fades. The need to prove, to push, to constantly strive—it softens. In its place comes awareness. Gratitude. A deeper understanding of what it actually means to live well.

I find myself reflecting on this journey—how everything has unfolded since the day I set out on February 28. Every destination. Every booking. Every connection. The timing, the locations—none of it feels random.

It feels guided. As if some greater force has watched from above and has been gently placing each piece exactly where it needed to be.

And choosing to end my time in the Algarve here, at the Conrad, feels like the perfect closing chapter—though not an ending, but a continuation. Because everything about this journey has aligned in a way that feels almost effortless.

As my final twenty-four hours approached, there was one more moment that reminded me just how powerful it is to stay open to life.

I had the pleasure of connecting with Ricardo, the hotel's marketing manager. Our schedules had made us nearly miss each other entirely. The connection almost didn't happen. But then, in one of those perfectly timed moments, I happened to glance at my email just after unpacking. There was a small window—just minutes before his next meeting.

And just like that, everything aligned.

We met in the lobby and made our way to the Nest lounge bar where we sat down to celebrate the release of my article on *Thrive and Travel.* It was a simple moment, yet deeply meaningful, sharing something I had created—not for recognition, but from a genuine desire to highlight what I believe is a true hidden gem.

Because that's the truth. I didn't write that piece to gain anything. I wrote it because the Conrad Algarve deserves to be seen, experienced, and appreciated for what it truly is.

And then came another unexpected moment. Ricardo presented me with a canvas Conrad bag filled with thoughtful gifts—towels, a bracelet, a sublimation cup. Completely unanticipated. Completely unnecessary. And yet, deeply appreciated.

I was appreciative not because of the items themselves, but because of what they represented: acknowledgment, connection, and the beauty of giving without expectation.

That's where the magic lives. Not in the grand gestures, but in the genuine ones. Not in what you can get, but in what you're willing to give.

And once again, it came back to the people.

The connections. The conversations. The relationships formed in the most natural, unforced ways. Even meeting another couple during my stay—beautiful people, not just outwardly, but from the inside out—reminded me how rich life becomes when you remain open.

Open to conversations.

Open to connection.

Open to possibility.

Because when you do, life responds.

It brings the right people into your path.

It creates moments you couldn't have planned.

It reminds you, again and again, what truly matters.

As I sit with these final moments at the Conrad Algarve, I don't feel like I'm leaving. I feel like I'm carrying something with me.

A deeper sense of peace.

A stronger awareness.

A renewed appreciation for the beauty of simply being.

And above all, a knowing . . . That when you trust the journey, stay open, and lead with intention, everything has a way of falling into perfect alignment.

Every time.

Chapter 31

THE SPACE BETWEEN DEPARTURES AND BECOMING

Leaving the Conrad Algarve wasn't just checking out of a hotel—it felt like saying goodbye to family. The farewell was bittersweet.

As my car transfer pulled up, I found myself embracing staff members who, in just a short time, had become part of my journey in a meaningful way. There were hugs, warm smiles, and waves goodbye as I stepped into the car. For a moment, I felt the weight of it—the kind of sadness that only comes from experiencing something truly special.

But deep down, as with other times in life when you want to linger just a little longer, I knew that I needed to keep moving. The next chapter was waiting. And my story still needed to be written.

As I made my way to the airport, I found myself in deep, meaningful conversation with my driver—one of those unexpected, beautiful exchanges that seem to happen when you're open to them. We spoke about India, about life, and about what brought him to the Algarve. There is something endlessly fascinating about people—their cultures, their decisions, their journeys. It's in these conversations that you begin to understand the true richness of life, not in places, but in perspectives.

I arrived early at Faro Airport, as I often do, waiting patiently for the departure board to reveal the TAP Air Portugal check-in counters. In

Europe, both at airports and train stations, there's always that moment of stillness before movement—nothing happens until suddenly everything does. (Flights are usually posted two hours before departure for the check-in counter number)

Once my flight was announced, I made my way to the premium counter, quietly grateful for the upgrade. My suitcase, now filled with gifts collected and received along the way, tipped the scale at 70 pounds.

"Just on the acceptable amount—perfect," the agent said.

I smiled. After thirty-four years of travel, I've learned how to balance it all—quite literally. My luggage scale has become one of my most trusted tools. It's funny how something so small can carry so much value.

Security, however, had other plans. I was flagged. Then my carry-on was flagged. I paused, mentally scanning what could possibly be the issue. The new shoes? Something I had overlooked?

No. Just one of those moments.

As I waited at the end of the screening belt, I found myself behind a British family—mother, father, and their son, who reminded me so much of my own. There was a moment of realization as the son said, "Oh no, I forgot to pack my liquids in my suitcase."

The mother—Mum, as they say in the Commonwealth—let out a frustrated sigh. "They'll take them now."

The father, calm and measured, gave his son a choice. "Do you want to go back through the line, since you didn't empty your water bottle, or leave it behind?"

I admired that. Not frustration, not judgement, not control—just guidance.

I gently spoke up to the son, "It's okay, these are the learning lessons of life."

The mum sighed again, "Yes, a very expensive one."

And in that moment, I felt called to say what I've come to understand more deeply on this journey. "I know, but when you put life into perspective, you have each other, and your health. That makes you very blessed."

There was a pause. A shift. A quiet realization. "Yes . . . Thank you. Safe travels."

And just like that, another connection—brief, but meaningful. There are no small encounters.

I made my way to the airport lounge, grateful for a moment of comfort: food, a glass of something refreshing, a quiet seat. Then the announcement came on the message board. Delayed. Then again. And again. Three times.

But this time, something was different. There was no frustration. No urgency. Just acceptance. Gratitude, even.

Because while others gathered in crowded spaces, waiting for gate announcements that would come much later (usually 45 minutes before the flight) I had a place to sit, to reflect, to just be.

Eventually, it was time.

At the gate, we waited for the outdoor tram that would take us to the plane—a reminder that travel, in its truest form, is not always glamorous. It requires patience. Strength. Endurance.

And then came the stairs. Twenty of them. No smooth walk down the gangway.

With carry-ons in hand, lifting, balancing, and moving upward. (Travel is not for the weak. It requires comfortable shoes, long walks in airports, and strength to carry luggage upstairs).

In that moment, I thought about all the older travelers I had seen along this journey. The falls. The injuries. The risks we don't often think about until we witness them. And it became clear. Travel while you can.

Don't wait for retirement. Don't wait for perfect timing. Because life doesn't promise either.

I found myself oddly grateful for my 70-pound suitcase—it had taken the burden off my carry-ons, making that climb just a little more manageable.

Lisbon greeted me with movement.

Energy.

A shift.

As my suitcase—clearly marked "heavy" and "premium"—made its way toward me on the belt, I felt that familiar transition from one chapter to the next. I ordered a BOLT ride and stepped into the SUV, immediately aware that I was no longer in the calm of the Algarve.

This was the city. Faster. Louder. Alive in a different way. But then, as if perfectly timed, I glanced out the window and saw these words:

"Today is your day."

A quiet message. A reminder. A choice.

Arriving at my next hotel—another Curio property—I was met with a different energy. Not the same warmth. Not the same attentiveness.

"I just gave my last suite upgrade away two hours ago," the front desk agent said. "You should have gotten here earlier."

I smiled politely, knowing full well that even if I were flying the plane myself, that would not have been possible.

And in that moment, I had a choice. To compare or to accept. I chose acceptance.

Now, sitting at a small table in my room, typing these words, I find gratitude in the simplicity of it all. A welcome drink was offered, and despite the late hour, I made my way to the bar. I placed my order—only to find they were out of what I wanted.

And again . . . a choice.

In that moment, I realized the crackers I had tucked away from the airport lounge were exactly what I needed. Paired with a glass of wine, they became enough. More than enough.

I won't pretend my heart didn't drift back, even briefly, to the Conrad Algarve—to the way they made me feel, like a princess, like I mattered. But this experience . . . . this contrast . . . didn't make me shrink. It expanded me.

Because life isn't about perfect moments—it's about how we move through the *imperfect* ones. And as I sit here now, I know this chapter is just as important as the last. Because growth doesn't happen in comfort.

It happens in transition. And this is where becoming begins.

Chapter 32
WHEN THE DAY OPENS ITSELF TO YOU

Do you know that feeling when everything just flows effortlessly? When events fall into a perfect pattern and you glide along with it in exquisite harmony? Today was one of those days—and it was magical. I'm still processing it, still sitting in awe of how naturally everything unfolded.

I set out on my own walking tour—no agenda, no pressure—just me and the rhythm of Lisbon guiding the way. The sights, the aromas, the sounds, the movements of people. This city moves to a gentle, layered rhythm. It's in the clatter of trams climbing narrow hills, the echo of footsteps on patterned stone sidewalks, and the rise and fall of voices drifting from cafés. Fado melodies spill softly from doorways, melancholic and slow. It's a blended city rhythm that sets the tone: unhurried, nostalgic, and quietly alive.

For the third time, I found myself standing beneath the Rua Augusta Arch, the grand neoclassical triumphal arch that connects Commerce Square to the bustling Rua Augusta street—and yet it felt entirely new, as though I was seeing it for the very first time. That's the beauty of returning to a place when you've changed—your experience changes with you.

From there, I wandered toward Pastéis de Bacalhau, indulging in what can only be described as one of the most delectable bites—warm cod cakes paired with a smooth Portuguese white port. It was simple, yet indulgent. Grounded, yet elevated. A perfect reflection of Portugal itself.

But the real magic happened in the in-between.

On my way there, I met an incredible artist—one of those unexpected encounters that shifts everything. For the past two visits, always accompanied by others, I somehow never found what I was truly seeking: raw, authentic art from Lisbon. But today was different.

Today, I was alone. Had I been with others, we likely would have agreed upon places to visit. But traveling solo gave me independence, and with that independence something opened. There was no outside influence. No agenda. No compromise. Just freedom.

Freedom to explore.

Freedom to pause.

Freedom to *feel.*

And in that space, I found it—the richness I had been searching for all along. Not just in the art itself, but in the experience of discovering it on my own terms.

When I returned to the DUO Hotel Lisbon, something shifted again. What had initially felt misaligned suddenly transformed. I was awarded an upgrade—one that changed not just the physical space, but the energy of the experience. In that moment, I no longer felt like I was navigating around discomfort or questioning recognition. I felt *at home.*

And it wasn't about entitlement—it was about *alignment.* About standing in what you've earned, what you deserve, and not shrinking to accommodate anything less.

Just like that, Sara entered the picture and elevated everything. Her kindness was genuine, her attention thoughtful, and her care for my schedule and workflow was evident. It wasn't forced—it was felt.

And I knew. Things were turning.

Then came another unexpected layer of connection. Through a mutual introduction, I was connected with Mauro—a true Portuguese soul who embodied the humility and depth of the culture. We arranged to meet at Lero Lero Wine Bar, and I'll be honest—I wasn't quite sure what to expect.

As I walked in, there was a moment of uncertainty. The energy felt unfamiliar, almost confusing. I paused, taking it in, wondering if I was in the right place. And then—there he was. Sitting near the entrance, he greeted me with a calm, welcoming presence that instantly grounded the moment.

And I remember thinking, *Wow, I thought this was a wine meeting*—but it was so much more than that.

Before I even had time to settle in, the space transformed into something extraordinary. Locals began gathering, and suddenly, I found myself in the middle of a live cultural experience—a poetry reading.

For the next thirty minutes, passionate voices filled the room. Raw. Emotional. Honest. The room felt hushed and attentive, with listeners leaning in to catch the spoken words. There were moments of silence, soft laughter, and gentle applause.

The culture was rich, and what struck me most was the age of the writers—so young, yet so deeply aware. They spoke about gratitude, honesty, and tough subjects like the realities of racism within neighborhoods. There was no filter, no performance—just truth.

You could feel their passion—not just in their words, but in their hearts, in their expressions, in the way their souls came alive as they spoke.

I didn't understand every word. But I felt every emotion. And I was in awe. Such incredible talent. Such depth. Such courage. I felt honored—truly honored—to be part of something so immersive, so genuine, so beautifully human.

And then, as if that wasn't enough . . . The night continued.

I had the opportunity to dine with Mauro and his daughter, sharing a meal that transcended language. While she didn't understand my words, she understood something deeper—my energy, my presence, my gratitude for the young woman she is and the woman she is becoming.

Because some things don't need translation. They're universal. And once again, I was reminded . . . This life—this nomadic journey—it's not about the places.

It's about the people.

It's about the culture.

It's about the connections we make along the way.

Yes, money makes the world go around. We need it. It supports our survival, our movement, our ability to explore. But it doesn't feed the soul.

Connection does.

Shared moments do.

Presence does.

And today . . . today fed my soul in a way I will never forget. As I sit here reflecting, I feel nothing but gratitude.

For the experiences.

For the people.

For the lessons.

Because this journey continues to show me, again and again, what truly matters. And for that . . . I am, and will always be, deeply grateful.

Chapter 33
THE CURRENCY OF CONNECTION

As I near the close of my time in Lisbon, I find myself in complete awe—not just of the city, but of the continued, undeniable theme that has followed me throughout this journey:

Connection.

Not surface-level encounters, but genuine, meaningful exchanges—stories shared heart-to-heart, invaluable lessons learned, rich cultures experienced rather than simply observed. It's as if every step I take draws me deeper into understanding what truly matters.

The day began with something simple—an Airbnb walking tour. Just two of us as guests, boarding the iconic Tram 28 alongside our guide. What unfolded over the next three hours was more than sightseeing.

We wandered through the charming, winding streets of the old town, where every cobblestone seemed to tell a story of those who had trod here before us. As we strolled, we couldn't resist popping into some of the historic churches that dotted the area, each one a masterpiece of intricate architecture and quiet reverence. From the ornate details inside the Church of São Sebastião to the stunning *azulejos* (decorative tiles) adorning the walls, we marveled at the craftsmanship.

In the heart of this lively, historic district, we took a well-deserved break to indulge in one of Portugal's most beloved treats at Manteigaria, an iconic pastry shop known for its exceptional *pastel de nata*, the Portuguese custard tart. The warm, golden pastry shell was perfectly crisp, its delicate layers offering a satisfying crunch with every bite. Inside, the custard was rich and velvety, sweet but not overwhelming, with a hint of vanilla and a subtle touch of cinnamon. The little cafe was cozy and inviting, with the scent of freshly baked *natas* filling the air—an experience that truly captured the essence of Portugal's vibrant food culture.

In that moment, we felt connected not only to the history of the city but also to the timeless joy of its culinary delights.

There's something about experiencing a place slowly, on foot, that allows it to reveal itself to you on a human scale rather than through the window of a tour bus.

By the end of the tour, I had clocked nearly four miles. My body felt it, but my spirit was energized. On my way back to the hotel, I stopped at Time Out Market Lisbon, grabbing a simple, hot Margherita pizza—nothing extravagant, just something grounding after a full day of movement and discovery. The gooey mozzarella cheese layered over rich tomato sauce and a flaky crust was just what I needed.

Back in my room, I answered a few emails, made a call to my airline, and allowed myself to lie down "just for five minutes."

We all know how that goes. Sleep found me quickly. But then—almost like a gentle nudge—I remembered that I had made plans. I had told Mauro I would attend his and Rita's wine tasting that evening at Vivants La Cave.

I could have stayed in. I could have told myself I was too tired, drawn a hot bath, soaked the day away, and called it a day. But something in me knew . . . This mattered. So I took a quick shower to refresh, got dressed, ordered a ride, and made my way there.

And it was, without question, the best decision.

From the moment I arrived, I felt it: that familiar energy of alignment. I connected instantly with Rita, not just as a person, but through her vision. Her wine brand, her label, her message—it all centered around women empowerment. It's a theme that has been deeply rooted in my own work since 2011.

And in that moment, it felt like more than coincidence. It felt like divine alignment.

What struck me even more was how this connection came to be. One person in Ft. Lauderdale. . . connected to someone in Italy . . . connected to someone in Australia . . . who knew someone in Chicago . . . who introduced me to Mauro and Rita.

Think about that. Different countries. Different lives. Different paths. All converging into one moment. That's what life is about. Not just where you go—but who you meet along the way.

This exemplifies the idea that our true worth is not measured by what sits in a bank account. It's measured by the relationships we've cultivated. That is the real currency of life.

And Rita's circle reflected that beautifully. Her friends—warm, open, vibrant—were a direct extension of her energy. It's never surprising when people who live with intention attract others who do the same.

At one point, one of her friends asked me a question that so many people wonder but don't always ask out loud: "Do you need money to start a nomadic journey?"

The answer is yes. Let's be honest—there is a financial component to stepping into this kind of life. Had I not bought and sold my home at the right time, I wouldn't be experiencing this 90-day journey at nearly fifty-seven years old.

But that's only part of the story.

Because what many don't realize is that this entire journey has been done on a budget. Every step. Every stay. Every decision. Yes, my thirty-four years in the travel industry have provided certain benefits, and I am deeply grateful for that. But those benefits are not the only way.

There are always options:

- Hostels.
- Long-term rentals.
- Housing search platforms for students, such as Uniplaces.
- Staying longer in one place instead of moving frequently.
- Being intentional with how and where you spend.

It's not about having unlimited resources. It's about having a willingness to begin, to take the leap. Because once you do, something incredible happens: You realize that while money supports the journey, it's the connections that define it and give it texture and meaning.

The conversations.

The shared laughter.

The moments of understanding between people who, just hours before, were strangers.

Those are the things that stay with you. Those are the things that change you.

As I stood there, surrounded by people from different walks of life, brought together by wine, conversation, and a shared openness to connect, I felt it again—that quiet knowing.

This is the richness of life. Not in what you own. Not in what you accumulate. But in what you experience. In who you meet. In how you show up.

And as my time in Lisbon begins to come to a close, I carry that with me.

Every lesson.

Every connection.

Every moment of awareness.

Because these aren't just memories. They are now woven into me, they have changed me, and they are part of who I am becoming. And for that I will forever be grateful.

Chapter 34
WHEN EVERYTHING CONNECTS

Today started exactly as I needed it to. No rushing. No overplanning. No pressure to follow every point on the "must-see" list.

I made a conscious decision not to book an excursion. I had to wake up very early the next day to catch a flight to Madrid. For the first time in this ninety-day nomadic journey, I wouldn't be alone. My dear friend (travel bestie) and hairdresser, Traci, would be joining me. We've traveled together before—different places, different chapters—and every time it's been filled with laughter, spontaneity, and unforgettable memories.

So, I knew that the next two weeks would be fun. Real fun. The kind that doesn't need planning. The kind that just happens.

I allowed myself a slow, leisurely morning. A late breakfast. A gentle walk down a quiet side street just taking in the sights and sounds, the sun warming my face, a soft breeze reminding me to stay present. There was no urgency—just ease.

And that's when the day began to unfold. Effortlessly. Right on cue, I received a message from Mauro. He had arranged a meeting—and not just any meeting, but one with the COO of Porta 6 Wine.

I paused. Because moments like this don't just "happen." They *build.* And to understand how I got here, you have to understand the journey behind it.

It all started back in 2018. A cruise ship. A chance meeting. A dapper Italian man who caught the attention of someone we lovingly called Blondie—another traveler who quickly became a friend. I stepped back, as life has a way of guiding those connections where they're meant to go, and over time, we all stayed in touch.

Fast forward to 2024. I found myself in Delray Beach, Florida, with Blondie. She arranged a small gathering, reconnecting us with that same Italian gentleman. What seemed like a simple evening turned into something much more—a referral to a friend in Italy connected to a winery.

Then, in March of 2026—yes, just a month before writing this chapter—The Italy connection provided another introduction to someone in Australia.

A woman who was on a mission to redefine positioning in the wine world. From the moment we met on Zoom, I knew. She was a kindred spirit.

She didn't just listen politely and hear me out—she shared and felt my vision. She understood the deeper purpose behind Burnt Out Party Girl Wine—the empowerment, the storytelling, the movement.

And just like that, in April, she connected me to someone in Chicago with a wine business. Two days before arriving in Lisbon . . . he connected me to Mauro.

Now here's where it gets almost surreal. My first day in Lisbon, I met Mauro at Lero Lero Wine Bar—a moment you've already read about.

What I didn't know at the time? He is the winemaker for Porta 6. My favorite Portuguese wine. The very same one I've purchased countless times at Trader Joe's. The same wine I've enjoyed, appreciated, and unknowingly been connected to long before this journey even began.

If you had told me in 2025, when I started building my wine brand, that I would one day be sitting in Lisbon discussing a potential co-branding opportunity between Burnt Out Party Girl Wine and Porta 6. I wouldn't have believed you. Not for a second.

It might have been improbable and even impossible—but for the power of connection: Kind-hearted people. Aligned energy. Unplanned moments that somehow lead exactly where they're meant to.

It's the confirmation that success is not a straight line. It never has been. It's a series of moments—some small, some significant—that weave together over time. And when you remain open, when you trust the process, when you lean into the unknown . . . that's where the magic lives and expands your horizons beyond what you ever dreamed possible.

Success takes a village. And in this moment, I felt deeply aware of mine. Every person. Every introduction. Every conversation. Each one played a role.

But there's one more layer to this story. Because nothing about this is a coincidence.

I had actually lost touch with Blondie for a period of time—until 2023. I made a simple Facebook post that I was heading to Europe. And just like that, she reached out.

"I'm staying in Lisbon. Come visit."

So, when I began my journey in Paris, I did something spontaneous. I left my luggage in my hotel room, packed an overnight bag, and took a quick flight to Lisbon.

Just twenty-four hours. That's all it took. We met at a rooftop bar. And something shifted. That was the moment I fell in love with Portugal.

What followed? It was even more remarkable.

Blondie helped me get my NIF—a tax ID that would allow me to buy property, open a bank account, and do business in Portugal. She guided me through steps that positioned me to one day live here. She opened doors I didn't even know existed.

And now . . . here I am.

All of my worlds colliding in the most beautiful way. Because if you had looked at my life on paper in December 2025, it would have told a very different story. Things felt uncertain. Unclear. Even bleak.

And then . . .

One decision.

One contract.

One house sale.

One moment of courage to trust the dream.

Paired with decades of experience in the travel industry.

And suddenly, everything aligned.

So, if you're reading this and you're standing on the edge of something big: A decision. A change. A leap that frightens you and makes you hesitate because you don't want to let go of the old and familiar even if that life no longer suits or fulfills you—let this be your sign.

Anything is possible.

Don't overthink it.

Don't wait for perfect timing.

Take the first step!

And trust that what is meant for you will begin to align in ways you could never plan. Because sometimes, the most extraordinary chapters of your life take flight with the simple decision to begin.

Chapter 35

FROM LISBON WITH GRATITUDE, TO MADRID WITH ANTICIPATION

It was time.

Time to say goodbye—at least for now—to Lisbon. Time to close one chapter and step into the next. As I made my way to the airport, I felt that familiar mix of gratitude and anticipation—grateful for everything I had experienced, and excited for what was about to unfold.

My Bolt driver, originally from Pakistan, and I quickly fell into conversation. We spoke about Portugal—how magical it is. He shared how much he loved the weather and the ease of life here.

And I smiled, saying, "Yes . . . But for me, it's the people."

Because it always comes back to that. The people.

When he dropped me off, I made my way to the TAP Air Portugal premium desk, quietly grateful for the upgrade. My seventy-pound suitcase—my now constant travel companion—felt a little less heavy knowing I had access to priority service. What I hadn't realized in Faro, but discovered this time through my own research, was that premium also came with Fast Track security, which is essentially the European version of TSA PreCheck in the U.S. It's a small detail—but a powerful one.

And a reminder: When you travel, sign up for text notifications with your airline. And if you're in a lounge and your gate hasn't been posted but boarding time is approaching—ask. The agents can scan your boarding pass and often give you the gate information up to an hour in advance.

These little things matter. Especially on a sold-out flight.

From Lisbon to Madrid, economy was completely full, and as expected, gate agents began tagging carry-ons due to limited overhead space. It's standard, even back in the U.S.—but in that moment, I was especially grateful to be seated in premium. Knowing Traci was already waiting for me at the airport, time mattered.

And yet . . . travel has its own rhythm. After my boarding pass was scanned, we were moved to one holding area. Then another. And another.

"Hurry up and wait," I said to the slightly anxious passenger behind me.

He laughed. "I like that. It's so true."

Indeed, it is. Travel teaches patience in ways nothing else does.

When it was finally time to board, that same gentleman helped me with my carry-on when the wheel caught awkwardly and froze. "Well done," he said with a smile. He was sharply dressed, polished—effortlessly so—and for a brief moment, I found myself wondering who he was.

But then something curious happened. He walked straight through the premium cabin. He didn't sit—just passed through.

We remained on the tarmac for over thirty minutes before takeoff. I found myself glancing toward the cockpit—and there she was. Our captain. A woman.

And I felt a quiet sense of pride. Because even now, that's not something you see every day.

Wheels up. Airborne. And just like that, service began.

The flight attendant approached and asked if I'd like some wine. "There are two selections," she said. "One from Alentejo and one from Dão."

I smiled. "I'll take the Alentejo."

She returned, not with a glass—but with the full bottle, presenting it as if I were seated in a private tasting. She explained the region, the characteristics, and the story behind it. Alentejo wines are rich, expressive, and versatile. Red wines from the region are typically bold with dark fruit flavors and a smooth, velvety texture, while white wines are fresh, fruity, and aromatic.

And just when I thought the moment couldn't get better, she encouraged me to try the Dão as well—"just to taste the difference."

Dão wines are known for their finesse, balance, and complexity. The reds are elegant, with dark fruit, floral notes, and smooth tannins, while the whites, especially made from Encruzado, are fresh, crisp, and aromatic.

It turned into my own in-flight wine experience. I felt like I was in a vineyard's tasting room rather than in the cabin of an airplane.

The flight attendant then shared that one of the wines was produced by the family of the first officer's wife, someone she followed on social media. She even wrote the name down for me, thanking me for the conversation and wishing me success.

Before she left, she asked about my brand—Burnt Out Party Girl Wine—and said she would be following my journey.

Another connection. Another reminder. It all matters.

As we landed and I deboarded, I texted Traci—knowing she had already arrived. Within minutes, I was at baggage claim, and as a premium passenger, my suitcase was the first to appear.

Smooth. Seamless. Except for one small detail. I was in Terminal 2. Traci was in Terminal 1.

Thankfully, I had prearranged transportation. And while my driver spoke only Spanish, my years living in Florida gave me just enough to communicate, to understand, to connect through a mix of words and hand gestures. We loaded my luggage, made our way to pick up Traci, and just like that—the reunion.

There's something special about traveling solo . . . but there's also something equally special about sharing the journey with someone who knows you—as Traci does me.

From there, we headed to our hotel—Preciados Hotel—a departure from my usual Hilton stays. No status. No expectations. Just trust. And once again . . . it delivered.

Early check-in. Room ready. Stunning décor. A perfect location in the heart of the city. Another reminder that sometimes, when you pivot for practical reasons—like cost—you're actually being guided toward something better.

After settling in, we grabbed a quick bite and toasted with a glass of sangria—Spain's signature welcome—known for its bright, fruity flavors and festive, easygoing vibe. Simple. Perfect. Exactly what we needed.

We both agreed that it would be an early night. Tomorrow would be full: a hop-on, hop-off bus tour, exploring the city, maybe even flamenco in the evening before continuing on to Barcelona. But for me, this moment held something deeper. A shift.

I had become accustomed to solo exploration—moving at my own pace, following my own rhythm. And now, I was stepping into shared space again. Smaller quarters. Shared decisions. A different dynamic.

But if there was anyone I could do that with, it was Traci: my travel bestie.

And just like that, a new chapter began. Not alone this time. But exactly as it was meant to be.

Chapter 36
TWENTY-FOUR HOURS IN MADRID—THE BEAUTY OF FLOW

Today was the perfect story of what twenty-four hours in Madrid can become when you allow life to unfold naturally.

Traci and I did something rare in travel. We didn't rush to the next adventure. We slept. Not just a quick rest, but a full, indulgent, luxurious eleven-plus-hour sleep. The deep, restorative sleep full of deep, vivid dreams. The kind that recharges and renews you.

It was not impromptu, it was intentional. I had purposely avoided booking anything early, remembering just how taxing the journey from the U.S. to Europe can be. I wanted Traci to land softly into the experience, to feel restored rather than rushed. And clearly, my body needed it, too.

When we finally eased into the late morning, there was no urgency—just a gentle start. We made our way to Starbucks for that much-needed jolt of caffeine, the kind that feels like it brings you back to life, sip by full-bodied sip.

From there, we headed to the city's hop-on, hop-off bus, agreeing we'd stay on and complete the full loop—a simple, easy way to take in the essence of the city.

But Madrid had other plans. At one point, Traci mentioned she'd like to stop near the Palacio Real de Madrid, the Royal Palace of Madrid, to grab something to eat. And yet, as the bus rolled on, something caught my eye—artwork along the street, a subtle pull I've learned not to ignore.

By now, I've come to trust that rhythm. That quiet calling. So, I turned to her and said, "Let's get off here and just walk."

And that split-second decision changed everything. We wandered without direction, allowing the streets to guide us, until we stumbled upon a place that felt like a gift—El Príncipe Restaurant. From the moment we arrived, the experience began.

We were greeted with complimentary Spanish champagne—unexpected, generous, and immediately setting the tone. Then came gazpacho, fresh bread, olives—a table that filled itself before we even ordered.

It felt abundant. Effortless. Aligned.

When our meals arrived, they were exactly what we hoped for—timely, beautifully presented, and satisfying in that way where you don't just eat, you experience.

We decided to order a full bottle of champagne, pleasantly surprised by how reasonable it was. There was no hesitation—just a moment worth celebrating. But what happened next . . . we never saw coming.

As we asked for the check, instead of simply closing out the meal and sending us on our way, they brought more—a lemon dessert drink, house-made cookies, and a digestive liqueur. No charge. No expectation. Just generosity and hospitality.

It was one of those moments where you pause and think: *This is what exceptional service feels like.* Unexpected. Thoughtful. Memorable.

This is a place I would recommend without hesitation.

From there, we made our way back to Hotel Preciados to refresh, soaking in the comfort of a space that had truly delivered on every level.

The complimentary minibar, the plush, high-quality towels, the blackout blinds that allowed for that deep rest, and beds that felt like sleeping on a cloud—it all added up to an experience that exceeded our expectations. The décor—elegant and elevated. The location—unbeatable— in the heart of Madrid in the vibrant and bustling Gran Vía area, one of the city's most famous and central streets, within walking distance of many major attractions, shopping districts, and cultural landmarks. And the service—consistent and warm from beginning to end.

Later, we headed out for one final highlight—sunset at the rooftop bar of Riu Plaza España. Standing above the city, taking in a 360-degree view of Madrid, it felt like the perfect way to close this chapter. The energy, the skyline, the golden light—it all came together in a way that felt almost cinematic.

And then, another connection. We met Anna. It was a simple conversation that turned into something more, as she shared that she had ties to a winery in another country. Once again, that thread appeared—that undeniable reminder that connection is everywhere when you're open to it. It never stops.

Back at our hotel, we ended our night at the bar, taking a moment to thank the staff for their incredible hospitality. Gratitude felt natural, not forced—because when service is this thoughtful, it deserves to be acknowledged.

As I sit here now, reflecting on the day, I realize how seamlessly Traci and I move together. There's no friction, no overplanning—just flow. And I am beyond grateful for that. Because travel isn't just about where you go. It's about how you experience it.

Tomorrow, we pack up and head to the airport—my now signature 70-pound suitcase in tow, somehow always working in my favor. Traci will be doing my hair once we arrive in Barcelona, and from there, a new chapter begins—a Princess cruise through Spain, France, and Italy.

But today . . . today was about Madrid. About slowing down. About trusting the moment. About saying yes to the unexpected. Because in the end, it's not the plans that define the experience—it's the in-between.

The conversations.

The surprises.

The connections.

That is the richness of life.

Chapter 37

THE JOURNEY BETWEEN DESTINATIONS

Today unfolded at a slower, more intentional pace—exactly what we needed. There's something about transition days in travel that calls for ease. Not rushing, not forcing—just allowing the moments in between destinations to carry their own meaning.

Traci and I started our morning by finishing up our packing, then heading out for one last bite in Madrid. We found ourselves at Prep La Crêpe, where we were greeted by a waiter who instantly lifted the energy of the room. He was jolly, warm, full of personality—the kind of presence that turns a simple breakfast into an experience.

And the food? Absolutely delicious. Perfectly made crêpes, thin and flavorful, and cappuccinos crafted with Colombian coffee—rich, smooth, and exactly what we needed to start the day. It was one of those small, unexpected highlights that stays with you.

Afterward, we made our way back to Hotel Preciados, wrapped up the last of our packing, and headed downstairs to check out. As we thanked the staff for such an incredible stay, they surprised us by asking for a group photo. That moment said everything. It wasn't just about service—it was about connection. And it left a lasting impression.

From there, we hopped into a Bolt and made our way to the airport, checking in with Iberia. I was pleasantly surprised to prepay for my now-signature 70-pound suitcase for just $38—an absolute win in the world of travel.

Once checked in, we headed to the lounge for a quick drink and a bite to eat before boarding. Or so we thought. Our flight was delayed—over an hour in total—and we found ourselves doing what every traveler eventually learns to master: waiting.

But even in the waiting, there was ease. We were seated together in a row of two near the front of the plane, which felt like a small luxury on a busy travel day. It wasn't until we landed in Barcelona that things took an unexpected turn: chaos.

There were no clear signs for baggage claim. No indication of which belt to go to. Just a sea of confusion and travelers trying to figure it out in real time. After a bit of searching, we turned to the internet where Google pointed us to Belt 0, where our flight number and Madrid origin were displayed. A small group gathered, waiting . . . all of us unsure.

Then I overheard something in Spanish—someone suggesting the luggage might actually be at Belt 15. One passenger sent his friend to check. Once confirmed, we followed. And that's when we met Eric.

Killing time while we walked, I casually asked him where he was from. "Orlando," he said.

I couldn't help but smile.

What are the chances? Meeting someone from the U.S.—from Florida, no less—right here, in the middle of a confusing airport moment in a foreign country, at exactly the right time.

Originally from the Dominican Republic, Eric spoke fluent Spanish and English, bridging the gap for us effortlessly. Together, we navigated what turned out to be an even more complicated path—walking a distance, passing through another security entrance, asking multiple staff members for directions.

And then finally, there they were: our bags.

Relief.

As we stepped into the elevator, something prompted me to start singing "Happy Birthday" to Eric—playfully, spontaneously. He paused, smiled, and said, "Thank you! Today is actually my birthday."

Of course it was. Because that's how these moments work. Perfect timing. Perfect alignment.

Eric led us to the Bolt pickup area, and before parting ways, we exchanged phone numbers. He was genuinely touched to hear I'd be including this moment—*him*—in my book. And once again, the message was clear.

It's never about the destination. It's about the people. The connections. The unexpected moments that remind you you're exactly where you're supposed to be.

From the airport, Traci and I made our way to Hilton Diagonal Mar Barcelona—a return for me, nearly seven years after celebrating my fiftieth birthday there. Walking in felt familiar. Comforting. And the welcome? Exceptional.

We were greeted warmly and upgraded to the top floor with executive lounge access. Although the lounge was just closing, the bell staff quickly took our luggage upstairs while we made a last-minute dash down to see what we could catch.

Most of the offerings had been cleared. But as we headed back toward the elevator, a member of the front desk team appeared, stepping in with us and handing over two complimentary drink vouchers.

Just like that. Thoughtful. Timely. Elevated service.

We settled into our room, refreshed, and then headed down to dinner at Intermission Restaurant Barcelona—an immersive, Broadway-inspired dining experience unlike anything I've seen before. Red carpet. Curtains. Playbill-style menus. It wasn't just dinner—it was an experience.

And, as has become the theme of this journey, the night didn't end without connection. We met a couple from New York celebrating their 40th wedding anniversary, and another couple from Napa preparing to board a Celebrity cruise the following day.

Different stories. Different paths. All intersecting in one space, for one evening. The energy was warm, open, and effortless. The kind of night that reminds you how beautiful it is to live in the moment, to simply be present.

Back in our room, the night closed in the most personal way—Traci doing my hair, preparing me for the next chapter: our Princess cruise. And as I sat there, reflecting on the day, one truth continued to rise above everything else:

No matter where I go . . .

No matter what I do . . .

It always comes back to the people.

Because when you move through life with an open heart and an open mind, without expectation . . . everything aligns exactly as it's meant to.

Every time.

Chapter 38
PREPARING TO BOARD

From time to time, life asks more of you. More energy. More money. More sacrifice. It doesn't always mean more drama. Sometimes, it is simply something like showing up—steady, present—choosing intention over autopilot. That Saturday morning in Barcelona began like so many others on the surface: a beautiful setting, a polished hotel, the promise of a seamless travel day. But beneath it, there was something deeper unfolding—a quiet sense of anticipation, of stepping into something long-awaited.

At the Hilton Diagonal Mar, the breakfast buffet wasn't just a meal—it was a moment. Fatima, with her warm persistence and effortless hospitality, insisted we slow down. In America, we are often accustomed to being rushed in and out to make way for the next diner on the waitlist. Fatima offered us a dose of sanity, and a reminder about how to enjoy each delicious bite. "It's Saturday," she said, topping off mimosas with a smile that said she meant it. *Relax. Breathe. Receive.* For someone used to constantly moving, that simple encouragement felt almost radical to me.

In our society, we're often conditioned to believe that rest must be earned. We have to work X number of months to get our two-week vacation. We have to answer a few more emails even on the vacation because we need to be responsible. But sometimes, rest is simply meant to be accepted.

As the morning turned to afternoon, Traci and I shifted gears from stillness to logistics. The kind of pivot that once felt draining now felt purposeful. We were preparing to board our Princess cruise, on a mission to find our port for embarkation on the *Sun Princess*, navigating a maze of vague directions and conflicting information. Google offered a possibility: Moll Adossat Pier. Not certainty—just a lead. And sometimes, that's enough.

At the front desk, confirmation arrived in an unexpected form: Michelle from St. Pete, Florida. Same region as us. Same ship. Same moment in time. What are the chances? But this trip had been like that from day one—threads of alignment weaving through every experience, reminding me that even when life feels scattered, something meaningful is still connecting beneath the surface.

It always comes back to the people.

Transportation hiccups followed—ride prices climbed with every refresh. But even that had its lesson. A bell staff member quietly pointed us in a better direction: Uber was significantly cheaper in Barcelona. One small piece of insight, one moment of guidance—and suddenly, the stress eased.

Not everything requires force. Sometimes, it just requires *asking*.

Our driver was highly rated, but communication was limited. "Port A," he said confidently. But something didn't sit right. From the back seat, I double-checked. A few quick searches later, the truth surfaced: we needed Port E. A small pivot—but an important one.

Distraction dulls your instincts. Presence sharpens them.

We made it. The right dock. The right ship. A quiet victory that felt bigger than it should have. Because it wasn't just about boarding—it was about trusting the process, trusting the journey.

Once aboard, the rhythm shifted. Wi-Fi connected us back to the world, but more importantly, we were stepping fully into this experience. There was something symbolic about upgrading my band to Commodore level—recognition of years of work, of persistence, of staying in an industry I've given thirty-four years to. Through every high and low, every demanding season, every moment of doubt.

Tired at times? Sure. Broken? Not even close.

Dinner at Sabatini's was more than indulgence—it was a celebration. Of resilience. Of arrival. Of choosing to keep going even when it would've been easier to check out. Later, at O'Malley's Irish Pub, live music filled the space with something you can't manufacture—joy that's shared, not scheduled.

And that's the thing about moments like these: they don't happen in isolation. They happen in laughter. In conversations. In shared experiences that remind you why you said *yes* to the journey in the first place.

Mallorca greeted us with sunshine and possibility. From the open top of a hop-on-hop-off bus, the world felt expansive again. Colors brighter. Air lighter. The kind of clarity you don't find by pushing harder—but by allowing yourself to experience life as it unfolds.

The island, with its stunning coastline and rugged mountains, seemed to whisper of endless possibilities. The scent of blooming orange trees mingled with the salty sea air, and everywhere we looked, vibrant colors—whether the deep blue of the Mediterranean or the terracotta rooftops of stone buildings—invited us to explore further. It was as if the island itself was welcoming us to a world where time slowed down, allowing us to savor every beautiful, sunlit moment.

We wandered, we shopped, we laughed. No urgency. No pressure. Just presence.

Back on the ship, the day unfolded effortlessly—pizza at Alfredo's, plans for the evening, anticipation for Marseille. But what stood out most wasn't the itinerary. It was the connection. The stories shared. The ease of being with someone who understands the unspoken parts of your journey.

This chapter isn't just about preparing to board a cruise. It's about recognizing when you've arrived at a moment you once looked forward to—and allowing yourself to fully step into it.

Because sometimes, the most meaningful part of the journey isn't where you're going. It's realizing—you're already there.

Chapter 39
THE DAY I FINALLY CHOSE MYSELF

I'm not going to lie—today was rough.

Not the sentimentalized kind of rough day people post about online with pictures of sunsets and quotes about resilience. I mean genuinely rough. The kind where your chest is on fire every time you cough—which is frequent and shakes you to the core—your body aches from exhaustion, and your mind is so emotionally overloaded you feel like you're walking in quicksand and your head is filled with cement.

I had been sick for days with what I had self-diagnosed as borderline bronchial pneumonia. Somewhere between determined traveler and absolute disaster, I found myself in Marseille, France, trying to convince a pharmacist to sell me a generic Z-Pak without a doctor's prescription. Looking back, I probably looked half dead standing there, wheezing, trying to get my point across through broken French and in survival-mode desperation.

As bad as this was, physical sickness was only half of it. The emotional sickness was worse.

The "Last Supper Guy" I mentioned earlier in this book—JD—had somehow found his way back into my emotional orbit again, despite every instinct in my body telling me he shouldn't have access to me anymore.

Why, you might be asking, did I keep in touch with him? The simply put, complex answer is trauma bonding.

That phrase sounds clinical and maybe even easily solvable—until you live it. A trauma bond is a strong emotional attachment formed through cycles of affection, inconsistency, pain, comfort, rejection, and reward. It's when someone hurts you, then becomes the person you run to for comfort from the hurt they caused. Your nervous system gets trapped inside the cycle until chaos starts feeling like a connection.

JD had "been there" for me during some incredibly difficult periods of my life—until he wasn't. When it came time for me to move, when I was drowning in stress, packing bins, lifting heavy furniture, trying to hold my entire life together with frayed emotional rope, he was suddenly always "busy" and unavailable. His focus? Himself. While I was sweating through sorting and packing up my life, he was sweating in front of the mirror—at the gym.

I should have seen the truth then. Actually, if I'm being completely honest, I saw it long before that. I just didn't want to accept it.

Because toxic relationships rarely begin that way. They start with hope. With potential. With dreamy moments that convince you to stay long after your spirit starts quietly breaking.

JD slowly reduced our relationship to convenience. Friday nights. Sundays. Scheduled appearances in his life instead of genuine partnership. Then he would complain about even spending those days with me because he would rather be with his friends.

Everything eventually became more important than me.

Everything.

I spent holidays alone while he went on four guys' trips a year. I booked trips for us, paid for accommodations, organized experiences, tried to create memories—only to hear complaints about having to travel with me.

Imagine loving someone so deeply while simultaneously feeling like a burden in their life. That contradiction will destroy your self-worth—if you let it.

The worst part about emotional erosion is that it doesn't happen all at once. Nobody wakes up one day suddenly empty. It happens slowly. Quietly. In small moments where you begin abandoning pieces of yourself to keep someone else comfortable.

Don't be too loud.

Don't be too affectionate in public.

No PDA.

Don't be "too successful" or you'll "get a big head."

Don't shine too brightly.

Don't take up too much space.

Don't become too much.

By the end, I barely recognized myself.

And the terrifying thing is, I didn't even notice how much I had disappeared until I finally left.

My Great Aunt Ruby saw it long before I did. "Darling, he doesn't love you. He's just using you. You would be far better off without him."

At the time, I didn't want to hear her words. Now I realize they were one of the greatest acts of love anyone had ever given me: honesty.

Because hindsight has a brutal way of revealing what survival mode hides.

Before JD, I was thriving. I had confidence . . . dreams . . . momentum . . . joy . . . a sense of identity.

Somewhere across four years of emotional inconsistency, I lost pieces of all of those things. Little by little, I unraveled without even realizing it. That's the danger of trauma bonds: they don't just break your heart—they disconnect you from yourself.

Even after I left, the cycle continued. When I moved, he asked me to leave my belongings with him. Expensive furniture. Personal items. Attachments. Even then, instinctively, something inside me knew better. I knew if I left pieces of my life there, I might never see them again.

I remember offering to rent a room instead.

His response? "I don't want you forever."

That sentence should have been the ending. But trauma bonds don't end with logic. They end with exhaustion. And then . . . Awareness.

Boundaries.

Distance.

Choosing yourself enough times that your nervous system finally believes you deserve peace more than chaos.

A few days ago, he texted me: (over the course of seventy-two hours)

"I miss you."

"I want to date you."

"Goodnight. I love you."

But the moment I asked who he was going to the beach with for his birthday, everything shifted again. He refused to answer. Every question was suddenly met with:

"It's time for us both to move on."

"I don't want to see you again."

"But let's be friends."

That emotional whiplash is what trauma bonding does to your brain. One moment, you are loved. The next, discarded. Then reeled back in again just enough to keep hope alive.

Research explains that when the person causing your pain is also the person comforting you, your brain begins linking them to safety. You become addicted to the highs and lows because unpredictability activates survival responses wired deep from childhood wounds.

You stop seeing reality clearly. Instead, you hold onto potential. The good moments. The version of them you hoped existed permanently.

Separation can feel less like losing a person and more like losing part of yourself. And in many ways, I did.

But this nomadic journey taught me something powerful: Not being together was the healthiest thing for me.

For the first time in years, distance allowed me to hear my own thoughts again. To reconnect with the version of myself that had been shrinking to fit inside someone else's comfort zone.

So today, while sick in France, emotionally exhausted and physically drained, I made one simple decision that may have changed my life more than any plane ticket, relocation, or fresh start ever could.

I blocked him.

No dramatic speech.

No final argument.

No begging for closure.

Just silence. A boundary. A decision to finally stop abandoning myself in hopes someone else would choose me.

Healing is not a destination. It's a process filled with grief, setbacks, clarity, loneliness, rediscovery, and rebuilding. Some days still hurt. Some days your nervous system misses the chaos simply because it was familiar.

But *familiar* does not mean *healthy*.

And loneliness is far less dangerous than losing yourself.

For years, I kept saying *yes* to everyone else while saying *no* to myself.

Today, I finally reversed that.

Today, I chose me.

Chapter 40
THE LESSON BENEATH THE HEARTBREAK

As I lay in bed coughing through another sleepless night, I tossed and turned replaying his words over and over in my head like a song stuck on repeat.

Isn't that what heartbreak does? It turns your mind into a cold interrogation room, where every memory, every conversation, every act, gets examined and then cross-examined under harsh fluorescent lighting. Every sentence becomes evidence. Every moment gets revisited looking for the exact point where things broke apart.

Or maybe the exact point where you abandoned yourself trying to keep someone else.

The deep coughing fits came in waves, rattling my chest while emotional exhaustion settled into my bones. It was a one-two punch. Somewhere between sickness, heartbreak, and exhaustion, I realized something painful:

I couldn't make sense of his behavior because I would never treat someone that way myself. When you love deeply, loyalty feels natural. Consideration feels natural. Partnership feels natural. So, when someone repeatedly chooses themselves at your expense, your mind searches desperately for explanations because emotionally healthy people don't naturally understand emotional selfishness.

"Classic narcissist," one of my friends said.

Maybe. Maybe not. At this point, labels almost don't matter anymore. What matters is how the relationship made me feel. Small. Confused. Uncertain. Emotionally starved. Unchosen.

And love should never leave someone consistently feeling unchosen. Those two things are completely incongruous.

The truth is, he should have stayed single from the very beginning. And I should have walked away the moment I realized we wanted completely different lives.

I wanted partnership. I wanted my life partner. I wanted someone to build with, dream with, travel with, grow with, and go through life with—not someone who treated commitment like a limitation on their freedom.

I wanted depth. He wanted independence disguised as a relationship.

While I dreamed about building a meaningful life together, he remained focused on appearances, validation, what people thought of him, his social life, his friends, and protecting his freedom at all costs.

His final words said everything I had spent years trying not to see clearly: "I long to be single, travel by myself or with my friends, go to concerts without you or anyone to answer to."

That isn't partnership. That's single life wearing the costume of commitment.

And finally—finally—I stopped trying to translate his words into something softer than what they actually meant.

People reveal themselves through patterns, not potential.

One of the hardest realities to accept is that sometimes we fall in love with who someone *could* be instead of who they repeatedly *show themselves* to be.

And if I'm being truthful, my grief isn't only about losing him. It's about losing time. I'm fifty-six years old. That realization hit me hard as

I stared into the darkness of this tiny room, listening to myself coughing into the night, replaying the tapes in my head.

Twenty years. Twenty years spent between two men who carried the same emotional patterns wrapped in different packaging.

Different faces. Different stories. Same outcome. Emotionally unavailable. Self-focused. Unable to offer the depth of love I was starving for.

That realization could easily become bitterness if I let it. But somewhere in the middle of the grief, another truth quietly emerged:

I still have time.

Time to live fully.

Time to love correctly.

Time to experience joy without shrinking.

Time to stop begging for breadcrumbs from emotionally unavailable people.

Time to become the fullest version of myself again.

And perhaps that is what this nomadic journey was truly about all along. Not escape. Awakening.

Because distance has a way of revealing truths you cannot hear when you are trapped inside familiar routines and emotional noise.

I regret shrinking myself.

I regret staying too long.

I regret communicating with him during this journey when, deep down, I already knew the relationship had expired emotionally long before it officially ended.

But regret can either imprison you or educate you. I am choosing education. Because the lesson underneath all of this pain is crystal clear now:

Stop giving your energy to people who do not value it.

Stop auditioning for love. Stop trying to convince someone to choose you.

Stop confusing inconsistency with passion.

Stop mistaking emotional starvation for chemistry.

Real love does not require you to disappear to keep it.

And for the first time in years, I can finally feel the beginning of freedom replacing attachment.

No more pullback.

No more emotional confusion.

No more waiting for texts that determine my worth for the day.

No more twisting myself into someone smaller just to remain lovable to someone incapable of meeting me fully.

Now I can follow my dreams completely.

I can travel freely.

Create freely.

Love myself fully.

Laugh loudly again.

Take up space again.

Become visible again.

And somewhere out there is the kind of love I spent years trying to force from the wrong people.

A grounded love.

A peaceful love.

A reciprocal love.

The kind of love that doesn't punish you for shining.

Maybe that person will come. Maybe they won't. But either way, I will never again abandon myself trying to earn love from someone unwilling to give it genuinely, freely.

That is the lesson in all of this. Not that I was too much. Not that I was unlovable. But that I stayed too long in places where my love was being mishandled.

And now? Now it's finally time to choose differently.

Chapter 41

EVERYTHING FALLING INTO PLACE

The last two days have been an absolute whirlwind.

One moment, I was wandering through the charming streets of Corsica, soaking in centuries of history, beautiful coastlines, and bustling open-air markets, and the next I found myself standing in the middle of Genoa, Italy, staring at a massive line wrapping around the hop-on-hop-off bus station.

Travel has a funny way of teaching you patience whether you want the lesson or not.

The line was long, the station crowded and chaotic, with frustrated tourists fanning themselves trying to stay cool as they baked in the Italian sun. At first glance, it looked hopeless. People were grumbling about sold-out tickets, delayed buses, and hour-plus wait times.

Then somehow, almost by instinct, Traci and I noticed a small sign advertising skip-the-line bracelets. We jumped on it, and within minutes, we discovered we had purchased the last two available bracelets for the coastline bus tour. The last two.

Later, we overheard other cruisers saying buses were oversold and some passengers had waited nearly an hour and a half just to board because the buses were completely full.

Moments like what we just experienced have started feeling symbolic during this journey. I wouldn't call it luck, exactly, but rather alignment. As if life keeps quietly whispering: *Keep going. You're exactly where you're supposed to be.*

And while we stood there waiting for the bus, another incident happened that I still can't fully explain. A local Italian man walked slowly in front of me, locking eyes with me in a way that felt strangely intentional, almost as though he were delivering a message directly to my soul without saying a single word.

At that exact moment, my mind drifted back to the emotional toxicity of the night before with JD. The confusion. The finality of finally understanding that love should never leave someone feeling emotionally abandoned.

As the man walked past me, I glanced down at his shirt. It had three simple words: "You've got this." I froze for a second.

Maybe it was a coincidence. Maybe it was divine timing. Maybe it was simply the universe finding strange little ways to speak when your spirit is exhausted enough to listen. But in that moment, standing in a crowded Italian port feeling physically sick and emotionally drained, it felt like the reassurance I didn't know I needed.

You've got this.

Not "you had this."

Not "you almost made it."

Not "you lost everything."

You've got this.

Present tense.

As if life itself was reminding me that despite the breakup, despite the years lost, despite the fear of starting over at fifty-six, I was still standing.

Still breathing.

Still traveling.

Still healing.

Still becoming.

The coastline views were breathtaking. Italy has a way of making even ordinary moments feel cinematic. The architecture alone looked like artwork layered across cliffs and narrow streets, each building carrying stories older than anything back home.

For a few hours, I forgot I was sick. I forgot about the breakup. Forgot about exhaustion. Forgot about the heaviness I had been carrying emotionally for months. Travel does that sometimes. It gives your soul little pockets of oxygen.

After the tour, Traci and I made our way to an authentic Italian restaurant called Vegia Zena, a local favorite tucked away from the heavy tourist areas. The kind of place where you know the food will be incredible because the townspeople are the majority of the customers.

I ordered spaghetti carbonara and a local wine, determined to savor every bite slowly. There's something healing about authentic Italian food—simple ingredients prepared with care instead of excess.

For a moment, life felt normal again. Comforting, even. But the second we started heading back toward the ship, reality came crashing back into my lungs. The coughing started first. Then the rattling. Then the wheezing. Each breath was more labored and sounded heavier than the last.

By the time we returned to the cabin, I could feel the exhaustion settling deeper into my chest. We changed into pool clothes anyway, determined not to surrender the entire day to sickness. We sat in the sun for about forty-five minutes, letting the warmth hit our skin while the Mediterranean breeze gently swirled around us.

I kept hoping sunlight, vitamin D alone might somehow heal me. But deep down, both Traci and I knew something wasn't right. The previous night had been brutal. Two hours of sleep at most—and probably not consecutively.

The rattling in my lungs was so loud it kept waking me up throughout the night. Every wheeze echoed through the cabin like my body was waving a white flag I wasn't ready to acknowledge.

The antibiotics I had managed to get in Marseille—after convincing a pharmacist to sell me a generic Z-Pak without a prescription—clearly weren't enough anymore. Neither was the inhaler my pulmonary specialist back home had prescribed before I left.

At some point, stubbornness has to meet reality. So, we headed to the ship's medical clinic. And for the first time during this health scare, I finally felt genuinely cared for.

Thank goodness for my annual Travelex Insurance policy, which covered situations like this. Pay up front, file a claim later. Peace of mind while traveling internationally is priceless, especially nearly thirty days into a nomadic journey across multiple countries.

The doctor treating me was from Cape Town, South Africa, and believed strongly in integrative medicine, which immediately put me at ease. Instead of dismissing my natural approaches, she actually appreciated my background and my 4.0 GPA that earned me my degree in alternative medicine. We discussed the ways I had been supporting my body naturally over the previous three weeks while also acknowledging that sometimes holistic support alone is not enough.

Eventually, we both came to the same conclusion: Severe bronchitis with fluid in my lungs. And with a combined 12.5 hours of flights scheduled to get me back to Orlando on May 4th, we both knew my lungs needed stronger intervention quickly if I was going to travel safely.

The solution? A steroid prescription strong enough to finally reduce the inflammation and open my lungs before my return home.

Oddly enough, receiving that diagnosis brought relief. Not because I was excited to take steroids, but because uncertainty is exhausting. Once you understand what you're fighting, you can finally stop spiraling and start healing.

After the clinic visit, it was back to the cabin to quickly get ready for dinner at Sabatini's Italian Trattoria. A second night of incredible Italian food and wine.

At this point, Italy was slowly feeding both my emotional and physical exhaustion one plate at a time. For me, however, the real star of dinner wasn't the wine. It was an extra glass of nonalcoholic ginger beer infused with real ginger.

The doctor and I had both discussed circulation and inflammation earlier, and ginger naturally supports both. What amazed me most was realizing I had instinctively purchased authentic dried ginger—no sugar added—the day before from a local market in Corsica. Sometimes your body quietly knows what it needs before your mind catches up.

By the end of dinner, reality returned once again in the form of something far less glamorous than Italian coastlines and specialty restaurants: laundry. After nearly thirty days of international travel, my laundry situation had officially reached critical levels.

We made our way to the laundromat located on our ship floor—two washers and two dryers tucked into a tiny laundry room, with identical setups scattered throughout each deck of the ship. And apparently every single passenger had the exact same idea.

With many guests onboard for back-to-back seven- and fourteen-day cruises, those machines had become a hot commodity. Finding an available washer felt harder than securing reservations at a five-star restaurant.

The setup itself was surprisingly affordable: $1.50 for detergent. $3 to wash. $3 to dry.

But figuring out how to actually operate everything while exhausted and wheezing was another story entirely. Thankfully, another sailor stepped in kindly and showed me how to order detergent, locate the dispenser, and start the machine. And just like that, my laundry finally spun into motion.

Standing there watching my clothes tumble through the washer, I couldn't help but laugh quietly to myself. Because somehow, despite sickness, heartbreak, exhaustion, uncertainty, travel chaos, oversold tours, crowded ships, and sleepless nights . . . everything still kept falling into place exactly the way it was supposed to.

Not perfectly.

But purposefully.

And maybe that's what courage really looks like sometimes. Not having everything under control. But continuing forward anyway.

As time passed and the ship slowly settled into its nighttime rhythm, I realized my laundry mission was far from over.

Anyone who has ever traveled for an extended period knows that laundry eventually becomes less of a chore and more of a survival necessity. After nearly thirty days abroad, I had officially reached the point where re-wearing anything was no longer an option.

So when the washer timer was nearing completion, I practically sprinted back toward the laundry room determined to transfer everything into the dryer before someone else claimed the machine.

Cruise ship laundry rooms are no joke. With only two washers and two dryers per floor and thousands of passengers onboard, timing becomes an Olympic sport.

As I rounded the corner into the laundry room, I saw a male passenger standing directly in front of my washer with the door already open, clearly preparing to remove my clothes so he could use the machine himself.

I had made it just in time.

Breathless and wheezing slightly, I quickly pulled my damp clothes from the washer and loaded them into the dryer before anyone else could claim the spot. I set the timer for forty-five minutes, silently thanking God for small victories, and rushed back out.

Traci, meanwhile, wanted to make a quick stop at the casino and then swing by the main bar to say hello to one of the friendly passengers we kept running into throughout the cruise—a funny, easy-going woman from Pittsburgh who somehow always seemed to appear at exactly the right moments.

That had become part of the magic of cruise life: familiar strangers becoming temporary characters in your story. But as the minutes passed, I started getting anxious.

"Traci, it's time," I finally said. "I do not want that man removing my clothes from the dryer."

The thought of a stranger handling my laundry after nearly a month of travel somehow felt deeply personal.

So once again, I raced through the ship—first stopping at the cabin to grab my laundry bag before making my way back down the hallway toward the laundry room.

And there he was. The same man sat casually inside the laundry room, waiting.

The second he saw me, he smiled and said, "You have six minutes left."

With a laugh, I added, "Oh, my, hurry up and wait. My normal language."

Travel has a strange way of turning complete strangers into acquaintances through conversations you never saw coming.

We made small talk while waiting for the dryer countdown to finish. "Where are you from?" he asked.

"Florida," I replied before asking where he was from.

"Toronto."

What started as idle chit-chat quickly became something far more interesting.

He explained that he had been affiliated with the dentistry business for years but had shifted much of his focus toward investing in companies and entrepreneurial ventures.

Then came the sentence that made me pause. "I'm actually looking for a wine brand."

I almost burst out laughing. Seriously, what are the chances?

Here I was, exhausted, recovering from severe bronchitis, emotionally healing from the final break up, standing in a tiny cruise ship laundry room in the middle of the Mediterranean, suddenly having a conversation with a Canadian investor interested in wine brands of all things.

Life is strange and synchronous like that. Just when you think you're buried under exhaustion and uncertainty, opportunity quietly walks into the room disguised as an ordinary moment.

We exchanged numbers, and I texted him the information before finally pulling my warm laundry from the dryer.

As I folded clothes late that night, I realized something powerful: The more I release control and simply stay open to life, the more unexpected doors seem to appear.

Not every encounter is meant to become something huge. Some are simply reminders.

Reminders that life keeps moving.

That opportunities still exist.

That new people, new connections, and new possibilities can appear anywhere—even beside a dryer on a cruise ship somewhere between Italy and the next destination.

And maybe that's part of healing, too. Learning that after heartbreak, after loss, after disappointment . . . life still has surprises waiting for you.

Chapter 42

THE TRUTH *FINALLY* SET ME FREE

As I lay in bed wheezing and coughing through the darkness of the night and into the early morning pre-dawn hours, my mind replayed everything that had happened with JD like scenes from a movie I no longer wanted to watch but somehow couldn't turn off.

His words echoed over and over in my head.

"I miss you."

"I want to date you."

"I love you."

"I want to go my separate way."

"I long to be single and free."

"I can't commit to making positive changes."

This was not over a period of months. These came from him all within a matter of *days*.

Maybe that's what finally broke the illusion for me—not one statement, but the emotional chaos of all of them combined and the perspective that distance now offered me. Because those words weren't new. They were the entire four-year relationship pattern compressed into a single week.

Push.

Pull.

Love.

Distance.

Affection.

Rejection.

Hope.

Disappointment.

The jumble of conflicting scenarios came at me repeatedly until I became emotionally exhausted trying to stabilize something that was never emotionally stable to begin with.

But this time, something shifted. This time, when he said, "I can't commit to making positive changes," instead of trying to negotiate, fix, explain, or wait patiently for potential, I felt liberated. The truth finally set me free.

Because after years of promises, conversations, lack of apologies, temporary improvements, emotional backtracking, and repeated cycles, he had finally spoken the most honest sentence of our entire relationship.

He can't commit to change.

Not *won't. Can't.*

And there is a painful kind of freedom that comes when someone finally admits they are unwilling or unable to meet you where you've been begging them to stand for years.

As I stared into the darkness, listening to the rattling in my lungs, I started reflecting on all the stories he told me about his previous relationship. For years, I heard about how terrible it had been for him, how badly he had been treated, how everything was supposedly the other person's fault.

And not once—not once—did he acknowledge his own role in any of it. That should have been my red flag. Because healthy self-awareness sounds different.

The reality is that it takes two people to create relationship patterns.

No one is perfect. We all contribute something to the dynamic. We all have wounds, triggers, flaws, and lessons to learn. It takes two to tango.

And people continue repeating the same emotional cycles until they become self-aware enough to finally learn the lesson. I think I've finally learned mine.

Lying there in the dark, I found myself remembering the few things I genuinely liked about us. And that's the dangerous part about healing. The mind has a way of zooming in on positive memories while quietly editing out the parts that damaged you. The mind doesn't like that in-between stage, maybe because of the unknown about the future, so it clings to parts of the past, like holding on one last time before you let go and take the leap.

I remembered the affection. The hugs. The kisses. The comfort of physical closeness.

But then, slowly, the fuller picture returned. The constant verbal abuse. The dismissive brushing off gestures with his hands whenever I expressed hurt. The love-bombing through text messages only to show up in person emotionally disconnected and cold. The way he could speak lovingly one moment and cruelly the next.

And one sentence, in particular, still lingers heavily inside me: "I can treat people any way I want."

I remember staring at him after saying, "You can't treat people this way," genuinely shocked by the lack of empathy behind his response.

Those words will stay with me for a long time. Because they revealed something I spent years trying not to fully see: Some people know they are hurting others and simply don't care enough to stop.

That realization hurts differently. And deeper still, I realized something else that finally brought clarity.

He didn't love *me*.

He loved the *idea* of me.

He loved having someone there when it benefited him. Someone loyal. Someone supportive. Someone willing to accept breadcrumbs and still call it love.

And I became addicted to chasing those breadcrumbs. The occasional affection. The temporary tenderness. The rare moments where he became the version of himself I hoped was real and desperately wanted him to be all the time.

But love should never feel like emotional scavenging. Real love nourishes, even when times are difficult or you have inevitable disagreements. It doesn't starve. It doesn't make you question yourself.

Looking back now, the reflection feels strangely freeing. Because once you stop romanticizing the pain, you can finally see the truth clearly.

And the truth is, this relationship was never the great love story I kept trying to turn it into. It was not a movie. It was a lesson. A painful one. An expensive one, emotionally and financially. But still a lesson.

The positive memories don't mean I'm moving backward emotionally. They don't mean I should ever go back. They simply mean my attachment system hasn't fully caught up with my logic yet. And understanding that has changed the way I speak to myself during healing.

I've learned I need to gently separate two things: The physical affection—something I genuinely need and deserve—and the person who gave it. He was someone who also brought toxicity into my life. Those are not the same thing.

For a long time, my brain fused them together. The comfort. The touch. The kisses. The emotional highs.

My nervous system associated him with relief and reward, even while simultaneously associating him with pain. That's why trauma bonds feel so confusing. The physical closeness created something almost identical to a habit loop. My brain learned to associate him with temporary comfort, and now that connection is being broken.

And breaking it feels a little like withdrawal. Not because the relationship was healthy—but because inconsistency itself became chemically familiar.

What I'm feeling now isn't a sign to return. It's my body remembering something it liked without fully remembering the emotional cost attached to it.

And there was a cost. My confidence. My peace. My nervous system. My voice. Pieces of my identity.

Somewhere in the middle of the coughing, wheezing, and restless exhaustion of that night, I shifted position in bed and realized something unexpected: I felt relieved it was over.

Not devastated.

Not panicked.

Relieved.

For the first time in years, I no longer felt responsible for carrying on a relationship that one person was constantly trying to escape while still benefiting from my love. That relief felt unfamiliar at first. But it also felt honest. Because deep down, underneath the attachment, grief, and emotional withdrawal, I finally know something my friends and family have been trying to tell me for the last three years:

I deserve far better.

And maybe the biggest milestone in healing isn't when other people recognize your worth. Maybe it's the moment you finally stop arguing with them about it.

As I struggled through another laboring breath that morning, I realized something

I am still here.

Despite everything. Despite heartbreak. Despite illness. Despite loss. Despite all the moments I thought would break me. *I am still here.*

And because I am still here, I still have the opportunity to begin again. Suddenly, this no longer feels like loss. It feels like a clean canvas.

A chance to rebuild my life differently.

To get things right in all areas of my life.

To choose differently.

To love differently.

To stop settling for emotional survival and start creating actual peace.

What if this isn't the ending at all? What if this is the first honest beginning I've had in years? That thought alone feels liberating.

So now, moving forward, I want to use this opportunity wisely. No more shrinking. No more chasing breadcrumbs. No more forcing alignment where none exists.

Only truth.

Only authenticity.

Only what brings ease, flow, and joy.

The great teachers, writers, and visionaries all speak about it in different ways:

- Follow your bliss.
- Trust the flow.
- Choose peace.
- Honor your spirit.

And maybe courage isn't about endlessly sacrificing and enduring pain. Maybe courage is finally choosing joy after you've become far too familiar with suffering. That is the life I want now. And for the first time in a very long time, I believe I'm finally ready for it.

In the middle of all this reflection, another realization brought me an unexpected sense of peace: I am so grateful he had no idea where any of my belongings were stored, where I was staying, or the places I had traveled throughout this nomadic journey.

For once, I protected my privacy instead of overextending access in the name of love. That matters more than I realized at the time.

Maybe he feels like he "won" because he sent the final text. Maybe he believes walking away first somehow gave him power or control over the ending. But real power was never in the final message. Real power was in me finally reclaiming myself.

I kept my peace.

I kept my privacy.

I kept control over my own life.

And after years of feeling emotionally exposed, manipulated, and vulnerable inside the relationship, that realization is incredibly empowering. Because this ending was different.

This time, I didn't lose myself completely trying to hold onto someone unwilling to truly hold onto me. This time, I walked away with my future still fully in my hands.

Chapter 43
THE PEOPLE WHO HELP GUIDE US HOME

I think one of the greatest truths about being human is this: No matter how strong, independent, intelligent, or resilient we become, we all still need that one person we can reach out to when life becomes too heavy to carry alone.

The person who helps steady us when our thoughts become too loud.

The person who reminds us who we are when uncertainty clouds our direction.

The person whose presence alone feels grounding.

For me, that person is my spiritual teacher, Kate, who lives in the U.K. Before setting out on this nomadic journey, I reached out to her in search of clarity. At the time, I felt emotionally exhausted, spiritually disconnected, and deeply uncertain about where life was leading me. And somehow, with a calmness I still cannot fully explain, she laid everything out.

The emotional unraveling with JD.

The ending.

The emotional freedom that would eventually follow.

The travel.

The uncertainty.

The transition.

The reinvention.

She even gave me a timeline.

And now, sitting here reflecting on the past several months, it's almost unsettling how accurately everything unfolded exactly as she said it would.

So, in many ways, none of this feels shocking anymore. Painful? Absolutely. But shocking? No, definitely not. Sometimes, I think our spirit already knows when a chapter is ending long before our heart is willing to accept it.

Today was our scheduled Zoom meeting, and I had been looking forward to it more than I realized. Not because I expected her to magically solve everything for me, but because talking with Kate always brings me back to center.

There's something incredibly comforting about speaking with someone who sees beyond the temporary chaos and reminds you of the bigger picture unfolding underneath it all.

So, there I was—sitting in my cruise ship cabin somewhere off the coast of Italy, preparing to return to Florida on May 4th, laptop open, the waves of the ocean quietly moving outside my window, speaking with my spiritual teacher in the UK about the complete unraveling and rebuilding of my life.

If someone had told me a year ago this would be my reality, I would never have believed them. And yet here I am. Somewhere between heartbreak and reinvention. Somewhere between endings and beginnings. Somewhere between exhaustion and expansion. A sort of emotional purgatory but not in a bad sense, but more the turning of a page.

We talked about everything:

Career.

Relationships.

Friendships.

Family.

Purpose.

Fear.

Healing.

The future.

And by the end of the conversation, as always, I felt lighter. Not because all the answers suddenly appeared, but because calm returned to my nervous system. That alone is priceless.

Florida no longer feels like home to me anymore. It feels more like a temporary place to rest my head before the next chapter fully reveals itself. And honestly, that realization is both exciting and terrifying. Because now the uncertainty is becoming very real.

My ninety-day nomadic journey officially comes to a close at the end of May, and the questions are starting to grow louder:

Where do I live?

What comes next?

What kind of life do I truly want to create?

What does "home" even mean now?

And perhaps the biggest question of all: How do I finally manifest the life partner I've been longing for instead of repeating old emotional patterns?

That question feels different now. Less desperate. More intentional. Because I no longer want love born from loneliness, attachment wounds, or emotional survival.

I want aligned love.

Peaceful love.

Grounded love.

A partnership where I do not have to abandon myself in order to remain loved.

And then there's the career side of my life expanding rapidly at the exact same time everything else is shifting: the repositioning and expansion of the Burnt Out Party Girl wine brand. When I created it, I never could have imagined what would follow. What began as a bold concept born from reinvention, resilience, and starting over unexpectedly led to one of the most surreal creative moments of my life—the opportunity to co-write the brand anthem "B.O.P. Girl" with five-time Grammy Award winner Trae Pierce.

As someone who has always loved pop, R&B, and hip-hop music, this collaboration felt deeply personal and incredibly full circle. Music has always been one of the greatest emotional connectors in my life, and to watch an idea transform into a professionally released song alongside such an accomplished artist was a moment that felt oh so real.

What an absolute honor it was to release "B.O.P. Girl" and watch the Burnt Out Party Girl movement evolve into something far bigger than I ever imagined—a brand rooted in courage, healing, reinvention, empowerment, and learning how to celebrate life again after burnout.

There were tremendous growth opportunities surrounding the B.O.P. Girl anthem song. The endless creative possibilities. The pressure. The decisions. The timing.

It feels like every area of my life is simultaneously demanding transformation. And if I'm honest, sometimes it feels overwhelming. So many choices. So many unknowns. So many paths I could take.

And time suddenly feels louder now. At 56, near turning 57, you become acutely aware that your energy, time, peace, and purpose matter deeply. You stop wanting to waste years on the wrong people, the wrong places, or the wrong versions of yourself. You start craving alignment instead of survival.

That's why conversations like the one I had with Kate matter so much. Because in the middle of the storm, she brings calm.

Not fantasy.

Not avoidance.

Not false promises.

Just perspective.

A reminder that uncertainty does not mean failure. A reminder that endings create space. A reminder that life often falls apart right before it reorganizes itself into something far more aligned.

As our Zoom call ended and the screen went dark, I sat quietly in my cabin for a few moments listening to the soft hum of the ship's engine as we moved through the Mediterranean. And suddenly, despite all the uncertainty surrounding me, I felt something unexpected:

Trust. Not certainty. Trust.

Trust that I survived things I once thought would destroy me.

Trust that the wrong relationship ending is actually protection.

Trust that reinvention is possible at any age.

Trust that my future still holds beauty I cannot yet fully see.

Maybe that's what guidance is truly supposed to do. Not tell us exactly what to do every step of the way. But remind us that even in moments where life feels untethered, we are still capable of finding our way home to ourselves.

Chapter 44
THE TRUE MEANING OF LIFE

Today, the Sun Princess floated quietly off the coast of Santa Margherita Ligure, a picture-postcard perfect Italian seaside town with colorful buildings tucked against the coastline and hills rising behind it like a painting.

Because the ship could not dock directly at port, passengers had to tender ashore using smaller transport boats. As we watched them moving back and forth across the water, packed tightly with travelers, I couldn't help but laugh because they looked exactly like oversized yellow submarines, like from the cover of the Beatles album, bouncing across the Mediterranean.

The lines were crowded, the boats full, and honestly, after the last several weeks emotionally and physically, Traci and I looked at each other and made the decision to stay on board instead of doing a shore excursion.

And for once, choosing rest felt like wisdom instead of missing out. So, while thousands of passengers rushed toward another excursion, we spent the day slowly enjoying the ship itself, which we felt like we had to ourselves—the pool, the spa facilities, the warmth of the sun against our skin, and the rare feeling of not needing to be anywhere except exactly where we were.

Sometimes, healing looks like movement and destinations. Other times, healing looks like stillness and staying put.

While standing in line at the burger stand later that afternoon, life once again reminded me how powerful unexpected conversations with strangers can be. Here, I met a fellow passenger named Cyndi, who was originally from Canada. At first, it was casual small talk, the kind travelers exchange every day. But within minutes, our conversation shifted toward nomadic living, and suddenly I found myself deeply drawn into her story.

Cyndi told me she began her nomadic lifestyle journey at the age of fifty-eight, after devastating loss changed the course of her life forever. She had lost her husband at sixty-two to a rare form of brain cancer. Then, a short time later, heartbreak struck again when her son died at age forty-seven from the exact same disease.

The weight of those words settled heavily between us. And yet somehow, despite unimaginable grief, there was lightness in her spirit. She seemed at peace.

Now nearing eighty years old, she explained that years ago she had a very small house built in Canada— not a grand home filled with possessions, but a simple space she refers to as her "launch pad." It was a place to return to between adventures. A place that allowed her freedom rather than trapping her in maintenance, debt, clutter, or obligation.

Then she said something that stayed with me deeply: "I buy nothing when I travel. My memories are stored in my mind."

I immediately felt the truth of those words. So much of modern life teaches us to collect things. More possessions. More accumulation. A bigger house to put all the accumulated things. More storage when even the house won't hold it all. The souvenirs we buy to remember someplace we visit often get shoved into a drawer or the back of the closet, forgotten, which is totally ironic.

Sadly, somewhere along the way, many of us stop collecting experiences.

Cyndi spoke passionately about embracing nomadic living while we are still physically able to experience it fully. "Do it while you're young enough to enjoy it," she said.

And honestly, that has become one of the recurring themes of this entire journey. Because the truth is, none of us know what is around the corner. Life changes in an instant. Health changes. Relationships change. People leave. Circumstances shift. The future is never guaranteed.

And perhaps that's why experiencing other cultures, meeting people from all walks of life, hearing their stories, tasting different foods, walking unfamiliar streets, and opening ourselves to connection is the true richness of life.

It's definitely not the stuff. It's not the mumus or the pookah shells from Hawaii. It's not the beret and the Louis Vuitton bag from Paris. It's not the leather gloves and the Murano glass from Venice.

It's the moments.

The conversations.

The perspectives.

The expansion.

Cyndi's story reminded me that reinvention does not expire with age. You can lose everything and still rebuild meaning. You can grieve deeply and still choose adventure. You can simplify your life and somehow become richer spiritually because of it.

Afterward, Traci and I ended up spending time by the pool again with our Pittsburgh friend, whose familiar presence had become one of those small comforts aboard the ship. It's funny how quickly cruise life creates temporary little communities. People you may never see again somehow become woven into your memories forever.

Eventually, we returned to the cabin to get ready for our dinner reservation at The Catch by Rudi followed by an evening theater performance onboard. There's something surreal about watching live entertainment while floating through the Mediterranean Sea, knowing entire countries await outside your cabin window each morning.

And yet tonight carries a different energy. Tomorrow requires an early 7 AM disembarkment for a nine-hour excursion through Pisa and Florence involving coach rides, walking tours, and what will likely become another unforgettable chapter of this journey.

It will also be our last full day aboard the Sun Princess before ending this European adventure with two final days exploring Rome on our own. That realization makes me emotional.

Because somewhere during these weeks abroad, this journey stopped being just a vacation. It became transformation.

So many lessons.

So many twists and turns.

So many emotional unravelings.

So many connections made with strangers who somehow arrived exactly when they were meant to.

And through all of it, one truth keeps revealing itself over and over again: The true richness of life has never been found in possessions, titles, appearances, or perfection.

It lives in people.

In culture.

In conversation.

In connection.

In courage.

In experience.

In being fully awake to the life happening right in front of you, before time quietly slips away.

Chapter 45
THE SPACE BETWEEN STORIES

I woke up this morning with a kind of excitement that felt almost foreign in my body—like when you open up a room that had all the doors closed and the shades drawn and the sunlight and fresh air suddenly floods in. Today was supposed to be simple: a nine-hour excursion to Pisa, and to my favorite place in Italy, Florence. A place that has always felt like a return to something softer, something truer.

And yet, beneath that excitement, there it was . . . the ache . . . the echo . . . the quiet unraveling of something that was familiar, and that once felt like home.

Because healing isn't linear, no matter how beautifully we try to package it. You can be boarding a train toward joy and still feel the residue of what you left behind. Four years of attachment doesn't dissolve just because you made a brave decision. The body remembers what the mind has already released. The nervous system doesn't speak in logic—it speaks in sensation, in memory, in waves that rise when you least expect them.

This morning, mine was speaking loudly. Old reflections surfaced. Moments with JD I thought I had already made peace with came back—not to haunt me, but to be felt fully without resistance, maybe for the first time. There was a purge happening, the kind that doesn't ask for permission. The kind that reminds you: You can move forward and still need to release.

And for once, I didn't try to outrun it.

Before this trip, I made a decision that now feels like one of the most supportive acts of self-trust I could have chosen. I signed up for Gabrielle Bernstein's coaching program. Years ago, when she was on my radio show, something about her voice, her perspective—a grounded spirituality—stayed with me. She spoke about the universe having your back in a way that didn't feel like blind optimism, but like a deep, embodied knowing.

Today, it felt like that knowing met me exactly where I was.

I opened her Gabi AI chat and told the truth about how I was feeling. Not the polished version. Not the "I'm doing great, everything's aligned" version. The real one. The one that said, "I feel like I'm free falling."

And the response I received didn't try to fix me. It met me: *When everything familiar drops away at once, your nervous system screams, "I'm unsafe," even if your soul chose this reset.*

That line landed somewhere deep. Because that's the paradox, isn't it? You can consciously choose change—choose growth, choose yourself—and still feel completely untethered in the process. You still feel like something is wrong, when in reality, something is simply shifting.

Nothing was wrong with me. I was in the space between stories. A purgatory, of sorts, but not in a bad place. And maybe that's one of the bravest places a person can stand. Not in certainty. Not in closure. But in the unknown—without rushing to fill it.

The guidance that followed was simple, almost disarmingly so. Place one hand on your heart. One on your belly. Breathe in for four. Out for six. Whisper, *In this moment, I am safe.*

I did it. Not because it sounded profound, but because I needed something real. Something physical. Something that could interrupt the spiral and bring me back into my body.

And something softened. Not everything. Not all at once. But enough. Enough to remind me that safety isn't something we find "out there"—it's something we practice, moment by moment, internally, especially when everything feels uncertain.

The reframe came next, and it changed everything: *You didn't lose the path; you cleared the clutter so the real path can appear.*

I sat with that. How often do we interpret endings as failures instead of necessary clearings? How often do we label ourselves as lost when we're actually just waiting to be written? Because that's what this is. Not emptiness. Unwritten space. And unwritten space holds possibility, even when it feels like absence.

The truth is, I don't know exactly where I'm headed. Not in the neat, mapped-out way I once lived, trying to control every detail of every move. But I'm starting to trust that I don't need to know everything to take the next step. Right now, my only job is smaller than that: Create tiny islands of safety.

A breath. A walk. A nourishing meal. A single honest page written without performance. A conversation with someone gentle. These are not insignificant acts. They are signals—to the body, to the nervous system, to the self—that say: *I can hold myself.*

And that changes everything. Because when the body feels held, feels nurtured, the mind stops searching so desperately for answers. Clarity doesn't come from force. It comes from safety.

So when the panic rises—and it will—I'm learning to meet it differently. Not with fear, but with gratitude.

Thank you, universe, for taking this from me and guiding me toward what's next.

Not because it's easy to say. But because it opens something. Because it reminds me that this isn't an ending—it's a redirection.

And then, in the middle of all of it—when I finally told my son it was over for real this time—there was a message. Simple. Uncomplicated. Certain in a way I couldn't yet be for myself.

"God has better plans for you, Mum."

No long explanation. No analysis. Just truth, offered with love. And somehow, that landed even deeper than all the guidance, all the reframes, all the breathing exercises. Because it reminded me that even when I feel like I'm walking into the unknown, I am not walking alone. That there is a perspective beyond my fear, beyond my grief, beyond what I can currently see.

A better plan. Not a louder one. Not a more complicated one. Just . . . better.

And maybe the most comforting truth of all is this: I'm not lost. I'm being remapped.

So today, I'll walk through Florence not as someone who has it all figured out, but as someone willing to feel, to breathe, to trust the unfolding. I'll let the beauty of this place, filled with so much history and artwork of the world's great masters, meet me where I am—not where I think I should be.

And I'll remember this: The courage it took to choose myself did not lead me nowhere. It's leading me somewhere that matches that courage.

For now, that's enough.

More than enough.

Chapter 46
THE TERRIFIC TRAVELING ASHTRAY

Back in 2000, before my divorce, I visited one of my favorite places in the world for the very first time: Florence, Italy,

There are certain places that imprint themselves onto your soul immediately, and Florence was that for me. There is so much splendor and magnificence concentrated into a relatively small area. The architecture, the history, the beauty of the surrounding countryside, the energy flowing through the narrow streets—it felt timeless, romantic, artistic, and deeply alive all at once.

But what I remember most from that first trip wasn't the museums or the guidebook must-sees, it was a tiny family restaurant called Trattoria Buzzino. The wood wainscotting, arched doorways, simple furnishings and checkered tablecloths welcomed us along with the mouthwatering aroma coming from the kitchen. More than that, the moment I walked through the door, the owner treated me less like a tourist and more like a long-lost family returning home. Throughout the meal, he brought extra food, additional drinks, desserts, and little surprises—all "on the house."

At some point I remember thinking: *I physically cannot eat another bite.* I was so full I joked I needed a pillow, a blanket, and a wheelbarrow so someone could roll me out the door and back out onto the cobblestone streets of the city.

Then, as we gathered our things, stood up, and prepared to leave, the owner suddenly waved me back enthusiastically. "Bella! Bella! Wait! I have something for you!"

My first thought was: *Dear Lord . . . no more food!*

To my surprise, he returned holding an ashtray. I politely smiled and said, "No thank you, I don't smoke."

He laughed warmly. "No bella . . . look."

When I looked closer, I realized it wasn't just an ashtray. It was a hand-painted piece featuring his trattoria—complete with the restaurant's name, address, and phone number painted directly onto it.

Suddenly it became more than an object. It became a memory.

Over the years that followed, I moved seven times across three different states. Life changed. Relationships changed. Careers evolved. Entire chapters of my life came and went.

And through all of it, I carefully protected that ashtray. Wrapped carefully. Packed thoughtfully. I weeded out many things over the course of all those moves, but I never once considered discarding it.

Somewhere deep down, I carried the promise that one day I would return, both to Florence and to the restaurant. And eventually, I did.

In June of 2024, while traveling through Europe on my own, I made my way back to Trattoria Buzzino after nearly twenty-four years. Walking through those doors again felt surreal. Only this time, I learned that the uncle who had spoiled me over two decades earlier had passed away, and his nephew Alessandro had taken over the restaurant.

I shared the entire story with him—the food, the generosity, the hand-painted ashtray that had somehow survived decades of moves and reinvention. He smiled warmly—I imagine I wasn't the first customer who had the same experience—and recommended the truffle pasta dish. And honestly? It was incredible. So incredible that I later wrote a glowing review for the restaurant on TripAdvisor because some experiences deserve to be celebrated publicly.

Fast forward to today. As part of Traci and my nine-hour excursion through Florence and Pisa, we were given three hours in Florence to explore. And, naturally, there was only one place I wanted to take her. Back to Trattoria Buzzino.

The weather was nice, so we sat outside under the shade of an umbrella where we could take in the charming ambience of the streetscape and people watch. Traci ordered the lasagna while I returned once again to the truffle pasta I had fallen in love with during my solo trip. At one point, a tourist walking past the restaurant stopped and asked if the food was good.

Without hesitation I laughed and replied: "It was in 2000, then in 2024, and it still is going strong."

That answer apparently carried some weight because they stopped in their tracks and sat down immediately. Then three other couples who overheard us followed behind them. The power of authentic experiences and genuine recommendations still matters in a world full of algorithms.

Founded in 1844 and still family owned today, the restaurant carries the kind of history you can feel the second you walk inside. It is more than a business. It is a calling. It offers not just authentic, delicious food, it offers something that cannot be quantified: hospitality.

And when Alessandro greeted me this time with a huge smile, a hug, and the traditional Italian kisses on both cheeks, it no longer felt like returning to a restaurant. It felt like returning to a memory that had somehow stayed alive and was quickly rekindled after all these years.

So, if you ever find yourself in Florence—which itself feels like walking through living history—put Trattoria Buzzino high on your list. It sits near the famous Ponte Vecchio—or "the bridge" as many

Americans simply call it—lined with vendors, jewelry shops, artists, and some incredible gelato.

We also made our way to Cathedral of Santa Maria del Fiore, the breathtaking cathedral originally designed in 1334 by Giotto and completed in the 15th century. No photograph truly prepares you for seeing it in person. The scale. The intricate detail. The incredible artistry. It stands there as a reminder of what human beings can create when passion, vision, and purpose align across generations.

Eventually, we made our way back to the coach and headed toward Pisa to capture the iconic tourist photo pretending to hold up the Leaning Tower of Pisa. And honestly? Sometimes cliché tourist moments become the most fun memories.

Afterward, we shared a caprese salad and sipped on limoncello spritzes before rushing back toward the coach.

In true travel fashion, there was one final unexpected twist. Traci and I discovered we had been upgraded to flatbed seating on American Airlines for our return flight. Along with being able to stretch out and sleep horizontally, we were suddenly allowed to check two pieces of luggage each at no extra charge.

This was perfect timing because my luggage situation had officially become questionable. Despite my best efforts and diligence, apparently, two T-shirts and a leather purse somehow translated into my suitcase weighing well over the seventy-pound limit. Travel math works differently in Europe.

So, on impulse, we quickly purchased a matching luggage piece and a magnet before racing back onto the ship.

Then it became a whirlwind. Quick refresh and change of clothes. Rush to dinner. Running into friends packing their own suitcases. Final hugs. Final conversations. And just like that, our journey was ending.

But what struck me most as the day closed wasn't sadness. It was gratitude. Because the true beauty of travel isn't just the destinations. It's the connections.

People like our incredible tour guide Lumi—someone with such infectious energy and personality that within minutes you simply know: These are my people, my tribe. The kind of souls you remain connected to long after the journey ends through social media, messages, memories, and shared moments.

That, to me, is the real souvenir.

Not magnets.

Not handbags.

Not even the terrific traveling ashtray.

It's the people who leave fingerprints on your spirit along the way. And what an amazing takeaway from such a fruitful journey.

Chapter 47
FROM BOUGIE TO MISREAD

Today was a strange mix of total exhaustion and nonstop laughter—one of those travel days where everything is a blend that feels slightly chaotic, slightly surreal, and somehow unforgettable all at once.

Our alarms went off at 6 AM for our 8 AM disembarkment from the Sun Princess. After weeks of living out of suitcases, traveling through multiple countries, surviving emotional breakthroughs, bronchitis, excursions, laundry-room adventures, and endless movement, I felt every ounce of exhaustion in my body.

And apparently so did our luggage. When our driver picked us up at the port, the first thing he did was laugh at the mountain of suitcases we somehow accumulated throughout this European adventure. I didn't judge him for that. I laughed, too. Travel has a way of multiplying belongings despite your best intentions.

Fortunately, the minute we stepped into the car, all exhaustion temporarily melted away. The vehicle was stunning. First-class. Smooth. Elegant. It honestly felt like riding on a cloud. After weeks of coach buses, cruise cabins, crowded ports, and constant movement, the quiet luxury of simply sitting in a peaceful car with air conditioning felt oddly healing.

Eventually, we arrived at the Hilton Garden Inn Rome Claridge near the Colosseum area, and somehow, by pure luck or divine timing, our room was already ready for check-in. That alone felt like a miracle.

We quickly changed clothes, grabbed a bite to eat, and then began what turned into a very long walk through intense Roman heat toward the hop-on-hop-off bus stop.

By this point, Traci and I had entered that level of travel exhaustion where everything becomes funny simply because you're too tired to process anything normally.

The stop we chose to jump off at was for the famous Trevi Fountain. And let me just say this clearly: It was absolute chaos. Beautiful chaos. Historic chaos. Overcrowded tourist chaos with people snapping selfies at every step.

The fountain itself was breathtaking, but the crowds were shoulder-to-shoulder packed with tourists, cameras, tour guides, and pickpockets, whom we couldn't identify among the throngs but the signs warning people about them were everywhere.

Rather than turn away and go to someplace approaching normalcy, we did what every traveler dreams of doing in Rome when they are here. We paid two euros each, turned our backs to the fountain, tossed our coins over our shoulders while we made our wishes, snapped selfies, and then escaped to a shaded corner nearby to sit quietly for a few moments reflecting on the experience.

There was something oddly peaceful about that pause in the middle of so much noise. Then, naturally, we decided rooftop cocktails were the next logical step. As we made our way from the bus stop to the rooftop bar, something hilarious started happening. We kept running into fellow passengers from the cruise ship. Not once. Not twice. Three times in three separate groups.

At the bus stop.

Near the rooftop bar bathroom.

Even while instinctively wandering through the streets searching for a taxi later in the evening.

You might think, *Well, Rome was a port of call so this can't be that unusual.* It is. Here's what makes it so wild: The Sun Princess is enormous. Rome is massive. And none of this was an organized shore excursion. Yet somehow, in a sea of tourists from all over the world, we kept colliding with the exact connections we had made onboard. It started feeling less random and more like proof that certain people are simply meant to cross your path repeatedly.

Eventually, we returned to the hotel to get ready for what we thought would be one of the highlights of the evening: our reservation waitlist attempt at La Pergola inside the legendary Rome Cavalieri, A Waldorf Astoria Hotel.

We had done our homework beforehand and placed ourselves on the waitlist hoping for a miracle opening. When we arrived, however, things immediately felt uncomfortable.

The hostess couldn't even find our waitlist request initially and explained rather coldly that there was no availability. The energy felt dismissive from the beginning.

But when I briefly explained my background and that I was documenting my experiences through writing, everything suddenly shifted. She immediately escorted us to the outdoor bar area for drinks overlooking one of the most spectacular panoramic views of Rome imaginable.

And yet despite the breathtaking scenery, something still felt off. Traci and I both noticed it. We felt looked down upon, as though we somehow didn't belong there, which honestly was ironic because we had dressed beautifully in the best outfits we could possibly create from weeks of living out of suitcases—both clad elegantly in black, polished, classy, and appropriate for the setting.

Yet the atmosphere carried an undertone that quietly said: You are not our usual clientele. And for a moment, I found myself reflecting on how quickly people make assumptions based on appearance, energy, age, luggage, confidence, status signals, or whatever shallow markers they choose to value.

Thankfully, the energy shifted when Lorenzo, the bar manager, arrived. He was warm, professional, attentive, and kind. He carefully reviewed my allergies, took our drink order personally, and brought out beautiful complimentary hors d'oeuvres with genuine hospitality.

That single interaction changed the entire emotional tone of the experience. Because true luxury is not dining under sumptuous chandeliers hanging from the ceiling or sipping glasses of aged, expensive wine. It's how people make you feel.

After drinks, we headed downstairs to Uliveto for dinner. And once again, we initially felt completely unwelcome. At one point, it genuinely seemed as though staff were preparing to escort us out despite the restaurant being nearly empty.

Then somehow, once again, the atmosphere shifted the moment they learned I was a reporter documenting my experiences. Suddenly service improved. Suddenly we were attended to. Suddenly we mattered. It was fascinating and, honestly, a little disappointing to witness in real time. Still, we enjoyed the evening.

We ordered wine, main courses, and dessert. Traci treated us to sweets while I chose fresh berries paired with authentic ginger gelato, which felt perfect after weeks of battling bronchitis and inflammation.

But the strangest moment of the night was still ahead. After dinner, we returned upstairs to wait for our car service. It was déjà vu. The bell staff almost completely ignored us. When one finally acknowledged me, his tone carried obvious assumptions. He questioned why we were there, seemed skeptical of our presence, and then casually said: "Let me guess . . . you're waiting on your Uber?"

The insult landed immediately. Not because there's anything wrong with Uber—but because of the assumption behind the question. As if we couldn't possibly belong there otherwise.

What made the moment even more ironic was realizing the chef affiliated with La Pergola also had connections to a high-end restaurant at another hotel where I had previously been welcomed warmly and treated with incredible kindness.

Funny how luxury spaces can produce completely different energies depending on the people inside them. So, I calmly smiled and replied to the bellman: "No. We're waiting for our Mercedes."

And almost like a scene from a movie, our driver pulled up moments later in a vehicle that looked nearly limousine level. He stepped out immediately, opened our doors professionally, and welcomed us inside.

As we drove away, I glanced back through the window. The bellman had suddenly removed his decorated hat, placed it over his chest, and gave a slight bow of acknowledgement after realizing he had completely misjudged us.

And honestly? That moment said everything. Because bougie is not always best.

Status is not character.

Luxury is not kindness.

Appearances are not truth.

Even if I became the biggest celebrity on the planet, I would still choose genuine, down-to-earth people every single time. Because they are the people who keep the world moving smoothly. The people who treat others well regardless of status. The people who understand humanity matters more than image.

The real lesson of tonight is simple: Never—and I mean never—judge a book by its cover.

Because often the millionaire next door drives the old car, wears simple clothes, and moves quietly through the world without needing everyone else to validate their worth. That's usually exactly why they have money in the first place.

Chapter 48
I AM NOT EMPTY, I AM BEING REMAPPED

Today started out rough. Despite finally getting an uninterrupted night of sleep, I woke up feeling completely worn down. My body felt heavy, depleted, and my harsh, unrelenting cough was still raging full force despite every effort I had thrown at it over the past several weeks: antibiotics, steroids, lozenges, breathe oil drops, water, inhalers.

The one thing my body truly needed—and had not received enough of—was rest. One decent night of sleep wasn't going to cut it and today wasn't a rest day.

We had booked an excursion I had been looking forward to: making pasta with Nonna Marisa outside of Rome, and despite my lungs protesting every step, I was determined to experience it.

So Traci and I got ready, headed downstairs for breakfast at the hotel, and made our way outside to meet our taxi.

And that's when the travel chaos began. Apparently, our original taxi had somehow been accidentally scheduled for 11 pm instead of 11:30 AM We had to pivot, and Traci quickly ordered another through the Uber app.

The driver pulled up, rolled down the window, and said what we thought sounded like "Traci." We climbed in. "Traci?" he repeated.

"Yes," we answered in unison, confidently.

Then, as he began driving off, something in me instinctively paused. "Where do you have as the drop-off?" I asked.

"Trevi Fountain," he replied.

Immediately, I knew something was wrong. "No, that's not correct. What name do you have?"

This time, we heard him more clearly. He answered, "Jessie."

Obviously, not us. I laughed in disbelief as we turned around and got dropped back off at the hotel to begin the process all over again.

Round two. New taxi. New directions. New attempt.

Only this time, after arriving at what we believed was the correct location, we discovered we actually needed to take a train to Piana Bella di Montelibretti station.

At this point, all we could do was laugh and try to rectify the situation. So, Traci ordered another taxi. The driver arrived, took off, then suddenly realized he himself had the entered the wrong address in his GPS.

He canceled the trip mid-ride, re-entered the correct destination, drove us there . . . and, in a perfect example of Murphy's Law, still managed to drop us off at the wrong end of the station.

This meant we had to walk alongside a highway and then try to safely cross over. It didn't seem like a good plan, but what were we to do? Then we heard the driver from the pasta shuttle yelling at us from a distance to go back down, then go up twenty steps, then back down again.

And this—THIS—is why I say travel is not for the weak. Not the glamorous, Instagram version. The *real* version.

The sweaty version.

The confusing version.

The "I might collapse from exhaustion but we're still figuring this out" version.

And I was doing all of this with compromised lungs. At several points, the only things carrying me through were my inhaler and pure mind over matter.

Truthfully, the pace I had been pushing myself at physically was beyond what any doctor would recommend. But somehow, despite all the chaos, everything still aligned perfectly. Eventually, eight other travelers arrived from places including France, London, and Indiana, and together we boarded the "Pasta with Grandma" shuttle.

The drive took us about twenty minutes into the beautiful countryside town of Palombara Sabina, where we were greeted warmly by our host, Alina. She was absolutely wonderful.

Energetic.

Welcoming.

Passionate.

She first gave us a brief walking tour of the charming town. It is a picturesque place nestled at the foot of Mount Gennaro and is surrounded by olive and cherry trees. Then, we boarded the shuttle once more for a short three-minute drive to Nonna Marisa's home.

The moment the door opened, all the stress of the morning melted away. There stood Nonna Marisa with the most infectious smile and warm energy imaginable. She radiated love, and you could tell it was genuine. She embodied hospitality.

From the welcome drinks to the pasta lessons themselves, the entire experience felt magical. We donned aprons, rolled up our sleeves, and took charge of our wooden rolling pins. We learned to make bow-tie pasta, ravioli stuffed with spinach, and fresh fettuccine completely by hand. It was tactile and relaxing.

No rushing.

No pretension.

No performance.

Just tradition.

Connection.

Joy.

At one point, Nonna sent us outside to walk through her garden while she prepared the lunch table.

The garden itself felt like something from another era—peaceful, organic, alive—filled with beautiful flowers and an abundance of herbs and vegetables.

Nonna waved us back inside to find tables filled with bottles of wine and the beautiful dishes with the pasta we had helped create together. The pasta you buy from a box at the grocery store doesn't even come close to the deliciousness of fresh pasta. We dove into our creations with gusto, and three rounds of homemade pasta later, we were all completely full and emotionally content.

Then came one of the sweetest moments of the day. Earlier, I had noticed in the excursion group chat that it was Laurent's birthday. His wife, Carine, from Fuveau, a town in southwestern France, had surprised him with the entire experience down to a special celebration.

Suddenly, Nonna emerged carrying a special birthday cake with a candle glowing brightly on top. And together, all of us sang "happy birthday" in Italian—the song "*Tanti Auguri a Te*," which translates to "many wishes to you."

It was one of those rare human moments that feels almost too pure for modern life. Watching Laurent and Carine together was deeply moving. They were so clearly in love. So joyful. So connected.

I honestly couldn't tell who felt happier—Laurent celebrating his birthday or Carine watching him experience the surprise she had planned with so much love. Their energy filled the entire room.

And I realized yet again that what fulfills us most in life is rarely material. It's connection. Thoughtfulness. Presence. Love expressed through moments.

The meal ended with a shot of Nonna's homemade limoncello crafted from the gorgeous lemons growing directly from her own tree in the garden outside.

And honestly, that's why everything tasted so extraordinary. It was made with love. Fresh ingredients. Care. Presence. Things we experience far too rarely in today's rushed, digitally curated world.

The day wrapped up with Nonna signing copies of her recipe book while guests purchased homemade olive oil. We hugged her tightly, took photos together, and eventually our driver Roberto transported us all back to the train station, helping everyone figure out tickets back to Rome.

Along the way, Traci and I stayed connected with Laurent and Carine because from the very beginning, I had sensed there was something special about them. I noticed it the moment they stepped off the train that morning. Some people simply carry beautiful energy.

And during our conversations at the station, I discovered why: They deeply believed in loving yourself first. In working on your inner being daily. In constantly striving to become a better person emotionally, spiritually, and mentally.

Their philosophy mirrored so much of what this journey itself has been teaching me: Life is not truly about the excursion or even the destination. It's about the people who unexpectedly touch your soul along the way.

Tomorrow, I fly back to Orlando. And honestly? It feels sad, which is understandable after a big trip like this. But it is also a little strange because Orlando no longer feels like home. Not really. It feels more like a temporary resting point between who I was and whoever I am becoming next. And that uncertainty has been terrifying at times.

Thankfully, today I found comfort through guidance from Gabbi AI, who explained something that deeply resonated with me:

"It's okay to feel terrified when your nervous system has been stripped of its landmarks. Your body is asking for anchors while your soul welcomes the clean slate."

That sentence stopped me in my tracks. Because that is exactly what this season of life feels like. Every landmark I once relied on has shifted. Relationship. Home. Routine. Identity. Future plans.

And yet, underneath the fear, my soul quietly welcomes the blank canvas.

She reminded me to place my hand on my heart, take belly breaths, and repeat: "In this moment, I am safe."

Then she encouraged me to create four simple anchors that depend on no one else.

A walk.

Sunlight.

Breathing exercises.

Stillness.

And finally, a gentle prayer to release the rest to the Universe. So tonight, that is exactly what I'm doing. God, this is where I need You to take over. Because, as she beautifully reminded me:

"When your body feels held, guidance gets louder."

And maybe that's the lesson. Not needing all the answers immediately. Just trusting the next kind step.

"I don't have all the answers, but I can take the next kind step."

So I will. Because that has been the beauty and purpose of this nomadic journey all along: To clear away everything that no longer serves my highest good.

And that process is courageous. Not because it feels comfortable. But because it creates space for an entirely new story to reveal itself one breadcrumb at a time.

After all . . . I am not empty. I am being remapped.

And now, with thirty days of nomad life left to go, the next chapter begins stateside. First, two days in Orlando. Then off to Virginia to celebrate my son's birthday, reconnect with friends, and continue navigating this unfolding new version of life.

After that, it's back to Orlando again and onward to my birthday cruise with Traci. Because somehow, even in the middle of reinvention, healing, uncertainty, and emotional rebuilding, life still finds ways to hand us moments worth celebrating.

And maybe that's the point. Life doesn't stop while we heal. It moves with us. Alongside us. Stretching us. Teaching us. Reintroducing us to ourselves one experience at a time.

This journey has been so much more than travel.

- It has been grief.
- Freedom.
- Exhaustion.
- Connection.
- Release.
- Awakening.
- Expansion.
- A clearing away of everything that no longer fits so something more aligned can finally enter.

Thirty days left. Thirty more days of unknowns. Thirty more days of becoming.

And for the first time in a very long time, instead of fearing the blank page ahead . . . I'm beginning to trust it.

Chapter 49
CONCLUSION

If there is one thing this journey taught me, it is that sometimes life has to completely dismantle the existing version of you, the one that was simply surviving, so the version of you that is truly meant to live can finally emerge.

When this story began, I thought I was simply exhausted. Burnt out from years of overgiving.

Overextending.

Overperforming.

Overloving.

Overproving.

But somewhere along the way, I realized burnout was never the deepest issue. Disconnection was.

Disconnection from myself.

From peace.

From joy.

From alignment.

From the life I was truly meant to live.

I spent years shrinking to fit inside places, relationships, and expectations that were never designed to hold the fullness of who I was becoming. I abandoned my intuition. Ignored red flags. Confused inconsistency for love. Mistook survival for stability.

And like so many people, I kept moving into each day, silently going through the motions. Smiling publicly while quietly unraveling privately. Until eventually life stepped in and removed everything that no longer served my highest good. Not all at once. But piece by piece.

The relationship.

The illusion.

The emotional attachments.

The certainty.

The version of home I once knew.

Even the identity I had carefully built over decades.

At first, it felt terrifying. Like standing in the middle of an earthquake watching everything familiar collapse around me. But now, looking back, I understand something I could not fully see then: The collapse was not punishment. It was redirection.

This nomadic journey across oceans, countries, cities, ports, train stations, airports, rooftops, cruise ships, restaurants, markets, and moments became so much more than travel. It became remembrance.

I remembered what it felt like to breathe deeply again.

To laugh with strangers.

To trust my instincts.

To connect with people without masks or expectations.

To sit in stillness and hear my own soul again.

I learned that healing does not happen in one dramatic breakthrough. It happens in tiny courageous moments.

Booking the ticket.

Taking the flight.

Blocking the toxic person.

Saying no.

Resting.

Trusting.

Starting over.

Asking for help.

Choosing yourself repeatedly even when it feels unfamiliar.

I learned that trauma bonds can convince you that breadcrumbs are love. But real love does not require you to shrink. Real love does not punish your voice, your success, your joy, or your expansion.

Real love feels safe.

Consistent.

Peaceful.

Supportive.

And perhaps most importantly, I learned that being alone and being free are not the same thing.

For years, I feared losing people. Now I fear losing myself. That lesson alone changed everything.

Throughout this journey, people appeared exactly when they were meant to.

The spiritual teachers.

The fellow travelers.

The strangers who became mirrors.

The couples who embodied healthy love.

The locals who welcomed us warmly.

The conversations that shifted something deep inside me.

Again and again, life reminded me that the true richness of existence is found in connection.

Not possessions.

Not status.

Not image.

Not perfection. Connection.

To people.

To Purpose.

To presence.

To ourselves.

I also learned that reinvention has no expiration date. At 56 years old, society tells women to become quieter, smaller, safer, more invisible. But this journey taught me the opposite. This is the age where wisdom finally meets courage. The age where you stop living for appearances and start living for alignment. The age where you finally understand that peace is wealth.

And maybe that is why this book is called *Courageous: Burnt Out, Not Broken*. Because I was never broken.

Exhausted? Yes.

Wounded? Absolutely.

Heartbroken? At times completely.

But broken? Never.

Even during the darkest moments, there was always a small part of me still searching for the light.

Still hoping.

Still believing.

Still fighting for a better life.

That part of me is what boarded the plane. What took the cruise. What walked the streets of Europe coughing through bronchitis and emotional grief. What sat in quiet cathedrals praying for clarity. What kept writing. What kept dreaming. What kept choosing to begin again.

And now here I stand at the edge of a completely new chapter. Not with all the answers. Not with a perfectly mapped future. Not with certainty. But with something even more powerful: Trust.

Trust in myself.

Trust in my intuition.

Trust that what left was meant to leave.

Trust that what is aligned will arrive.

Trust that I no longer need to force, chase, beg, or abandon myself for love, success, or belonging.

This journey stripped my nervous system of its landmarks. But in doing so, it also stripped away illusion. And what remains now is truth. I do not know exactly where I will live. What opportunities will unfold. Who will enter my life next. Or exactly what the future holds.

But for the first time in a very long time, I no longer need to know every detail in order to move forward. Because courage is not having certainty. Courage is taking the next step without it.

So, if you are reading this while standing in the middle of your own unraveling, your own heartbreak, your own burnout, your own reinvention, let this be your reminder:

You are not behind.

You are not ruined.

You are not too old.

You are not too late.

Sometimes, the most beautiful chapters of our lives begin only after everything we thought we wanted falls apart. Sometimes, losing the life you planned is exactly what makes room for the life that is waiting for you. And sometimes, the bravest thing a person can do is release what no longer serves them and trust themselves enough to walk into the unknown anyway. One breadcrumb at a time.

So here's to the endings that freed us.

The journeys that changed us.

The people who touched our souls.

The dreams still waiting to unfold.

The clean slates.

The second chances.

The healing.

The expansion.

The becoming.

And here's to all of us learning that being burnt out does not mean we are broken. It simply means it's time to rebuild differently.

With ease.

With flow.

With joy.

With courage.

And finally . . .

With ourselves fully intact.

Epilogue:
THE JOURNEY HOME

As if the journey itself wasn't enough, the trip home became its own lesson in endurance, surrender, and divine timing.

Leaving Rome was anything but seamless. What should have been a straightforward departure turned into two separate shuttle transfers, navigating crowded pathways, and hauling luggage up and down at least twenty steps that felt more like a climb up Mt. Everest, with every breath a struggle.

My lungs were compromised, my body depleted, and yet there was no option but forward. Travel in its rawest form—like life itself—doesn't ask if you're ready. It simply moves—and you move with it, making adjustments as needed.

But then came a small moment of grace. That flatbed seat in business class—what we call first class stateside—felt like a reward my body had been begging for. The ability to stretch out, to rest, to simply breathe without being folded into a cramped space made every chaotic moment leading up to that point feel worth it—or so I thought. The journey still had more to teach me.

We experienced a delay sitting on the tarmac, time ticking away as connections grew tighter and uncertainty crept in. Then came Miami, and what I can only describe as a complete baggage and connection nightmare. We missed our flight to Orlando and were placed on standby for the last flight of the night at 10:30 PM.

Exhausted.

Sick.

Running on fumes.

We waited, hoping. Only to be turned down for a seat. At that moment, the only option left was surrender. We booked a hotel for what would amount to just four hours of sleep. Except even that didn't come easily. The hotel shuttle never showed. So there we were again—dragging luggage, walking farther than we should have, searching for a taxi just to get a few hours of rest before doing it all over again.

By 4:00 AM, we were back up, racing to the airport to try again. Somehow, thankfully, we made it onto the next flight. Back in first class, I sat quietly, mask on, trying to conserve every ounce of energy left in my body, unaware at the time just how serious my condition had become. (It wasn't until later that day, after finally arriving home and seeing my doctor, that I would be diagnosed with a collapsed lung.)

In the middle of all that exhaustion, something unexpected happened. A conversation. The kind that seems random in the moment but reveals itself to be anything but.

Seated next to me was Annette, a sixty-one-year-old Senior Vice President of a major company who had spent thirty-eight years building her career in the same industry.

Successful.

Respected.

Accomplished.

And quietly at a crossroads.

She shared with me that she had been struggling with the idea of retirement. “I don’t know if I’m financially ready,” she said. “I have an incredible team . . . I don’t want to let them down.”

So, I asked her a simple question: “What is your passion?”

And without hesitation, her eyes filled with tears as she answered softly, “My grandkids. As simple as it sounds . . . spending time with them, watching them grow.”

There it was.

Not a title.

Not a salary.

Not a position.

Love.

So, I gently asked her: “If that’s your passion, what can you minimize to follow that? And what if you got a difficult health diagnosis tomorrow? Would you wish you had retired?”

Tears streamed down her face. “I’m sorry,” she said, dabbing at her eyes.

I shook my head. “Don’t apologize. That just shows your tenderness. And that makes you a beautiful person.”

In that moment, there was no hierarchy. No titles. No status. Just two women having a real conversation about life.

I shared a brief version of my nomadic journey with her—the unraveling, the healing, the courage it took to walk away from what no longer served me.

Before we deboarded, she hugged me tightly. She followed my journey, wanting to read the book when it was released. But what she said next stayed with me deeply: “I wasn’t even supposed to be in first class. I got upgraded.”

I smiled and replied, “I wasn’t supposed to be on this plane.”

She paused, then said, "I'm going to take you as a sign in my life . . . to listen to the crossroads I'm facing."

And just like that, another connection. Another reminder. Another moment where life gently whispers through people, through timing, through circumstance:

Pay attention.

Because sometimes the delays, the missed flights, the exhaustion, the reroutes, the discomfort—all of it is part of placing you exactly where you're meant to be. Even if it doesn't feel like it at the time.

RESOURCES FOR THE NOMAD LIFE

Nomad Life Checklist: Preparing for Freedom with Intention

Stepping into a nomadic lifestyle isn't just about booking a flight and making lodging reservations—it's about creating a system that supports your freedom. The more you plan, the more peace you create for yourself and your loved ones.

Foundation and Legal Prep

- Secure **travel insurance** (comprehensive, international coverage)
- Establish or update your **will, trust, and executor**
- Add your executor to:
  - Hotel reservations (when possible)
  - Travel insurance policy
- Provide your executor with:
  - Storage unit locations and keys
  - Safe access and location
  - Copies of important documents and contracts
- Store critical documents in a **secure safe**
- Ensure all contracts are organized and accessible

Home Base and Logistics

- Rent a **UPS Store mailbox** for mail/packages
- Maintain a **permanent address** even if you use a friend's (for

insurance, registration, medical)
- Terminate utilities (electric, water, internet, etc.)
- Secure **property/storage insurance**
- Confirm **storage unit locks** are high quality
- Decide:
  - Where your car will be stored
  - Where seasonal items will be stored
- Keep a small set of essentials at a **trusted friend's home** for rotation

Financial Management

- Set all bills to **auto-debit**
- Create a **realistic travel budget**
- Monitor finances **daily**
- Understand your **credit cards:**
  - Foreign transaction fees
  - Travel perks
  - Notify banks of international travel
- Carry **backup payment** methods
- **Keep a record** of your credit cards' customer service numbers and your account numbers in case a card is lost or stolen

Travel Planning

- Pre-book major travel (flights, key accommodations)
- Research:
  - Visa requirements
  - Entry regulations
- Ensure **passport and Global Entry** are up to date
- Exchange some **local currency** before arrival
- Download and update **travel apps**
- Share itinerary with trusted contacts

- Have a copy of your passport in case it is lost or stolen

Health and Safety

- Refill medications (minimum three-month supply)
- Complete doctor and dentist appointments before departure
- Carry copies of prescriptions
- Know nearby hospitals in destination areas
- Check in **daily with a trusted person**
- Ensure emergency contacts all have each other's information

Packing and Luggage Strategy

- Use a **50-pound suitcase mindset:** pack intentionally
- Invest in **quality over quantity**
- Plan wardrobe for **multiple climates**
- Include:
  - Compression socks
  - Comfortable walking shoes
  - Layering pieces
- Keep:
  - Important documents **on your person in an anti-theft travel purse, crossbody bag, or travel document organizer**
  - Essentials in a carry-on
- Use a **luggage scale**
- Understand airline **liquid and carry-on policies**

Tech and Connectivity

- Bring:
  - All necessary charging cords
  - Adapters for international outlets
  - Portable chargers
- Understand your **cell phone international plan**

- Bring backup devices if needed
- Use tracking tools (AirTags, etc.)
- Indicate in your contact list people who are emergency contacts.

Lifestyle and Daily Living

- Identify **laundry access points**
- Plan for:
    - Healthy eating options
    - Grocery access
- Bring small comforts:
    - Travel candle (battery operated)
    - Streaming device (Firestick, Roku, etc.)
    - Pillow if needed for sleep consistency
- Pack glasses/contacts and backups

Mindset and Intention

- Think **extensively** for "just in case"
- Think **simply** for daily living
- Take your time—don't rush decisions
- Be intentional with what you carry—physically and emotionally
- Remember: freedom requires structure

Final Reminder

- You are not just planning a trip—you are designing a life.
- Prepare for the unexpected.
- Simplify wherever possible.
- And trust that everything you've put in place allows you to fully step into the experience.
- Because the goal isn't just to travel: It's to live freely—with peace of mind.

TRAVEL HACKS THAT CHANGE EVERYTHING

What pops into mind when you think about travel? Is it the dreamy photos taken at exotic destinations? Is it the fabulous food eaten leisurely at a sidewalk café or overlooking the sun-kissed beach? Is it the new friends made in faraway places?

Of course, these things are great and certainly possibilities for your highlight reel. But before you get there you have to consider the nuts and bolts that can make or break your experience: the *logistics.*

Because the truth is that travel—especially long-haul and nomadic life—can either feel seamless or completely exhausting. And over the years, I've learned that the difference often comes down to one thing: preparation.

Not overpacking.

Not overthinking.

But *intentional tools* that make your life easier.

These aren't just items on a to-do list—they are solutions. Quiet upgrades that remove friction so you can stay present in the experience instead of managing discomfort or stress that can lead to chaos quickly and even more stress.

Let's start with *organization*—the backbone of ease.

Clear, TSA-approved toiletry bags are non-negotiable. They don't just help you breeze through security; they keep everything visible, clean, and contained. No spills, no digging, no frustration. They double as everyday organizers, bringing structure to even the smallest spaces.

Pair that with packing cubes, and you've completely transformed how you travel. These allow you to categorize your clothing—daywear, evening pieces, underwear, workout gear—so your suitcase becomes your closet. You don't unpack. You simply *live.* And most importantly, they prevent overpacking because every inch of space has intention.

And speaking of intention—knowing your suitcase weight matters. A compact, digital luggage scale is one of the most underrated travel essentials. Small, lightweight, and easy to use, it eliminates the stress of overweight baggage fees before you even leave your room. No guessing. No surprises at the airport. No whipping out your credit card to pay for the excess and taking an unnecessary bite out of your travel budget.

Security is another layer of peace. TSA-approved luggage locks with simple combination dials provide both ease and protection. They're quick to use, durable, and give you confidence knowing your belongings are secure—whether in transit or stored.

Now let's talk about comfort in the air. Sitting for hours in a confined space can be exhausting, but there are small things that can help.

A memory foam foot sling is a quiet luxury that makes a massive difference. It allows you to elevate your legs, change positions, and reduce swelling on long flights. While it's not a replacement for getting up and moving, it absolutely supports circulation and comfort—especially for shorter legs.

Add in compression socks, and you've created a system that actively supports your body. The right pair should slide on easily and not feel overly restrictive, but still provide enough compression to help prevent blood clots and reduce fatigue.

And then there's your environment. Noise-canceling headphones are a game-changer. They allow you to block out cabin noise, crying babies, and distractions—creating your own personal sanctuary in the sky. Whether you're listening to music, watching a movie, or drifting off to sleep, they elevate the entire experience.

A phone holder may seem small—but it's powerful. Attaching easily to tray tables or seatbacks, it allows for hands-free viewing and eliminates the constant strain of holding your device. They are compact, versatile, and incredibly effective.

Then there are the thoughtful luxuries. A small glass shot glass might not be on most packing lists, but once you have it, you'll never travel without it. There's something about sipping wine from real glass instead of plastic stemware, even mid-flight, that elevates the experience and prevents more trash from going into the landfill. It's durable, compact, and yes—flight attendants notice.

And then there are those small, everyday necessities: ultra-thin folding reading glasses are brilliant. They fit flat into even the smallest purse, making them both practical and space-saving.

Now let's talk about power—because in today's world, staying connected is essential. A European travel plug adapter with USB and USB-C ports is a must. It allows you to charge multiple devices at once—laptops, phones, accessories—without juggling outlets. Especially when traveling across countries like France, Italy, or Portugal, this becomes indispensable.

Health and wellness while traveling is another level of preparation entirely. If you choose to wear a mask, finding one that allows you to breathe comfortably makes all the difference. A well-designed mask with memory foam structure can filter unwanted particles while still feeling wearable for extended periods. I even add a drop of essential oil for an added sense of calm and clarity.

And speaking of oils—when navigating different cuisines and environments, your body needs support. Digestive blends can help your system adjust to new foods, while natural immune-support oils act as a proactive layer of protection. Travel exposes you to new elements, and staying ahead of that curve is key.

Sleep, of course, is everything. Time-zone shifts can disrupt your entire rhythm, and having a reliable sleep aid that supports neurotransmitters and relaxation can be a game-changer. The goal isn't to knock you out, but rather to gently guide your body into rest so you can wake up aligned with your new environment. Because when you sleep well, everything else flows better.

And then there's one of the most overlooked travel upgrades: Your transfers and ground transportation. Always check private car services ahead of time. Read reviews. Compare pricing. Often, they are the same price—or very close to—a taxi, but the experience is completely different. Seamless pickup, professional service, and zero stress navigating a new location after a long flight.

It's not just about getting from point A to point B. It's about how you *arrive*.

At the end of the day, travel isn't just about movement. It's about how supported you feel along the way.

These tools, these systems, these intentional choices—they create space. Space to enjoy. Space to breathe. Space to be present. And if there's one thing I've learned through this nomadic journey, it's this:

Ease is not a luxury. It's a decision. And when you choose it—everything about your experience changes.

If you're looking to simplify your travel and support a greater mission, you can find these curated essentials through my travel blog, where a portion of support continues to empower abuse survivors.

Because even in the smallest details . . . purpose can travel with you.

For more travel convenience and solutions please visit https://thriveandtravel.com/must-have-travel-accessories/

ABOUT THE AUTHOR

Dawn Burnett is a 26-time award-winning web series producer and host, travel reporter, entrepreneur, author, songwriter, and creator of the Burnt Out Party Girl wine brand. Known for her fearless reinvention journey and authentic storytelling, Dawn has spent her career inspiring others to rise through adversity, reclaim their voice, and courageously pursue a life aligned with purpose, passion, and freedom.

A seven-time published songwriter, Dawn recently co-wrote the brand anthem "B.O.P. Girl" with five-time Grammy Award winner Trae Pierce—a surreal full-circle moment blending her love for pop, R&B, and hip-hop music with the empowering Burnt Out Party Girl movement.

In early 2026, Dawn sold her home, placed her life belongings into storage, and embarked on a transformational 90-day nomadic journey throughout the United States and Europe. That experience became the inspiration behind *Courageous: Burnt Out Not Broken,* a deeply personal story of healing, heartbreak, reinvention, burnout recovery, travel, resilience, and learning to choose yourself again.

In addition to her work in media and publishing, Dawn founded the Burnt Out Party Girl wine brand, which donates a portion of every bottle sold to RAINN, the nation's largest organization supporting survivors of sexual violence.

Dawn's inspiring story, creative work, and visionary entrepreneurial projects have been featured across hundreds of national and international media outlets, highlighting her global impact in publishing, branding, and advocacy.

To follow Dawn's journey, visit https://burntoutpartygirl.com, where you can read more about her nomadic travel adventures in real time, hear her music, learn more about her wine brand, and stay informed about her upcoming projects.